8 Broads in the Kitchen™

# BREAKFAST & BRUNCH RECIPES

from 8 Innkeepers of
Notable Bed & Breakfasts

D1314047

WALNUT
STREET
BOOKS

LANCASTER,
PENNSYLVANIA

## Acknowledgments

A number of people have helped us on our journey to publish this cookbook: Larie Engles who invited us to turn her kitchen upside down for a photo shoot; Mark Smith and Matthew Lovette, of Jumping Rocks Photography; Christian Giannelli, of Christian Giannelli Photography; Karen Seagrave, of KES Photo; and Jenna Strawbridge. Your keen eyes, technical prowess, and creativity have provided the luscious photographs found throughout the cookbook. Thank you all!

Design by Cliff Snyder

With love and gratitude, we dedicate this cookbook

to our supportive and enthusiastic families, friends, colleagues, and guests,

who have inspired us to create and to share our recipes.

# Table of Contents

Our Journey     6

A Word about Our Ingredients     7

Fruit: An Apple a Day     9

Muffins, Scones, and Breads: Batter Up     43

Sweet Breakfasts: Guilty Pleasures     83

Savory Breakfasts: Get Crackin'     123

Side Dishes: Sidekicks     185

Sauces, Toppings, and Condiments: Oh, My!     211

Drinks: Chilled and Heated     229

Recipe Index     236

About the 8 Broads in the Kitchen     253

# Our Journey

En route to an innkeeping celebration in 2008, two of us thought it would be fun to pool the collective resources of several of our innkeeper friends and create a blog. And so we did. Food! Friends! Fun!

Time went on, and we eight current and former innkeepers notched nearly 200 years of combined innkeeping experience. Add more than 200,000 breakfasts served to and enjoyed by happy guests. Factor in at least a half-million cookies munched by those who stayed in our inns. Stir in a creative streak and a daring vision. And you get "8 Broads in the Kitchen!"

Over the years, we have worked together, helping each other hone our culinary skills and taking them to new heights. To share our talents and recipes, we began giving food classes locally and at national innkeeping conferences.

And now we are offering you our second cookbook! We love sharing what we have learned and our passion for breakfast and brunch.

The eight of us have become close friends through the joys of creative cooking and baking, along with the blessings and challenges of innkeeping and life. Shared cyberspace and in-person hugs, tears, and laughter have cemented friendship among us 8 Broads.

We hope you will savor our recipes, inspired by our credo that beautiful, freshly prepared food from the finest ingredients is best shared with fabulous friends. Creating breakfasts with flare is an extension of our hospitality. The universal language of food opens doors, inspires conversation, calms restless souls, and often is just a good reason to laugh. Food bridges divides; it connects varying philosophies.

Food! Friends! Fun! The 8 Broads in the Kitchen hope you will join them in stirring up fun in the kitchen!

# A Word about Our Ingredients

**Brown sugar:** Light brown, unless otherwise noted.

**Butter:** Unsalted. We do not recommend margarine because it doesn't produce the same high-quality result, and it isn't good for you!

**Eggs:** Large, unless otherwise noted. We recommend that for pregnant, auto-immune-challenged people, and small children, you use pasteurized eggs, especially in recipes calling for overnight storage, as well as custards which do not cook at high temperatures for longer periods of time. You can find these eggs in the dairy section of your grocery store.

**Flour:** Unbleached and all-purpose, unless otherwise noted.

**Lukewarm water:** Under 110 degrees F so it doesn't kill the yeast.

**Oats:** Quick-cooking oats, never instant. If a recipe calls for rolled oats, they need to be *rolled* oats, not quick or instant.

**Oil:** Canola, rapeseed, or corn oil, unless we specify olive oil.

**Salt:** We recommend using kosher and sea salt—kosher for baking, sea salt for cooking and finishing.

**Sugar:** Granulated, unless otherwise noted.

**Size matters!** Pans are whatever size the recipe calls for. Other sizes will give different results. A 9-inch pie shell, for instance, will take 1½ times the amount of filling of an 8-inch pie shell.

# Fruit

## An Apple a Day

# Baked Apples

KATHRYN WHITE

*Serves 6*
*Prep Time: 15 minutes* ❧ *Baking Time: 30 minutes*

6 to 8 Honey Crisp, Granny Smith, *or* Fuji apples, peeled and cored, *divided*

6 tablespoons brown sugar, *divided*

cinnamon, *divided*

nutmeg, *divided*

¼ stick (2 tablespoons) butter cut into small bits, *divided*

heavy cream, *divided*

**Note:** *The number of apples needed to fill the ramekins will vary, depending upon the size of the apples. A large apple should fill one ramekin, but you'll need more apples if they're small.*

1. Preheat the oven to 350°.
2. Grease 6 (3-inch) ramekins with butter or spray.
3. Quarter each apple. Thinly slice each quarter. Divide the slices among the ramekins, stopping when each is about half-full.
4. Sprinkle the apple slices with brown sugar, cinnamon, and nutmeg. Place a couple of bits of butter on the slices.
5. Repeat with the remaining apple slices until they are just above the rims of the ramekins. Sprinkle with more brown sugar, cinnamon, nutmeg, and butter.
6. Place the ramekins on a baking sheet and bake for 30 minutes.
7. When finished baking, splash each with a tablespoon of heavy cream and serve warm.

I love living in south-central Pennsylvania where apples are a major crop. I'm like a little kid at the farm markets where I hover over each bin to determine which variety I'll try this week. I am especially drawn to tart apples, and since this recipe calls for brown sugar, a tart variety stands up well.

# Lemon Brandied Apples

DEBBIE MOSIMANN

*Serves 6*

*Prep Time: 7 to 10 minutes* 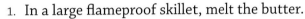 *Cooking Time: 15 to 18 minutes*

¼ stick (2 tablespoons) butter

4 large apples, peeled
and thinly sliced

zest and juice of 1 large lemon

3 tablespoons honey

3 tablespoons brandy

1. In a large flameproof skillet, melt the butter.
2. Add the apple slices. Sauté for 2 minutes.
3. Add the lemon zest, lemon juice, and honey. Stir together gently.
4. Cover and allow to cook until just soft, for about 10 minutes, depending on the apple type. Remove the skillet and apples from the heat.
5. In a separate small, flameproof pan, gently warm the brandy.
6. Carefully light it with a long match, being careful to stay away from drafts while doing so.
7. Pour the lighted brandy over the apples and allow the flame to burn out. Stir and serve immediately.

On a trip through Germany's Black Forest region, we had a meal in a spectacular old farmhouse that ended with the chef preparing these amazing apples tableside. They are perfect over cinnamon French toast, or, as he served them, topped with whipped cream and toasted almonds. Leftovers can be used to make muffins.

# Pomegranate Pear Salad, or Winter Fruit Salad

JOYCE SCHULTE

*Prep Time: 20 minutes*

ruby red grapefruit segments, peeled

sliced pears (choose one, *or* a combination of these varieties: Taylor, Comice, D'Anjou)

chopped fresh mint

pomegranate seeds

honey

1. Place sliced fruit, a little chopped mint, and pomegranate seeds into a fruit bowl.
2. Drizzle with honey, garnish with more fresh mint, and serve.

As an innkeeper, I always wanted to include a fresh fruit starter with breakfast each morning. I preferred something seasonal, and winter brought its challenges. Pears and apples were in abundance, but what else was out there?

Searching the produce aisles, I began to see many options. Citrus was in season, as were lovely "winter berries" like pomegranates.

Fresh mint was still available. And frankly, I really wanted a reason to always have lots of ruby red grapefruit in my kitchen. It's my favorite!

# Baked Apricots

YVONNE MARTIN

*Serves 4*
*Prep Time: 10 minutes* 🌿 *Baking Time: 15 minutes*

½ cup almonds

6 tablespoons brown sugar

3 tablespoons butter, at room temperature

20 apricot halves, plum halves, *or* peach quarters, fresh *or* canned

1. Preheat the oven to 350°.
2. In a food processor, combine the almonds, brown sugar, and butter just until well mixed.
3. Butter a 9-inch square baking dish. Arrange the fruit in the bottom.
4. Top with the almond/sugar mixture and bake for 15 minutes.
5. Serve warm, at room temperature, or chilled.

Serve this dish as a fruit course with breakfast or brunch, or fancy it up with a custard sauce, whipped cream, or ice cream for a light dessert. Since it has no flour, it's perfect for those on a gluten-free diet.

# Sunny Morning Citrus

DANIELLE HANSCOM

*Serves 2*

*Prep Time: 10 minutes* ❧ *Chilling Time: 1 to 8 hours, or overnight*

1 large pink grapefruit
(choose a firm one;
they're usually juicier)

2 large navel oranges
(again, pick firm fruit)

1 tablespoon honey,
*or* to taste

**Note:** *This recipe can easily be made for a crowd by multiplying the amounts of the ingredients.*

1. Peel the fruit with a sharp knife. Remove all the white pith to expose the segments. Hold each fruit over a medium-size bowl to catch the juice.
2. With a sharp knife, carefully cut between the membranes to separate the citrus segments. Let the segments fall into the bowl.
3. When done, gently stir in the honey.
4. Cover with plastic wrap. Refrigerate for at least an hour, or ideally, overnight.
5. Before serving, gently stir the segments. The honey will have melded with the juices. Distribute between 2 single-serving size glass dishes and serve cold.

*A refreshing winter breakfast fruit dish, this recipe's flavor improves when prepared and refrigerated overnight.*

# Poached Pears with Orange Glaze

ELLEN GUTMAN CHENAUX

*Serves 8*

*Prep Time: 35 minutes*  *Cooking Time: 55 to 60 minutes*

## For the Glaze:

6 navel oranges

cold water for cooking zest

4 cups water

3 cups sugar

½ tsp. salt

¼ cup orange liqueur

## For the Poached Pears:

4 cups water

4 cups sugar

¼ cup freshly squeezed
lemon juice

4 Bosc pears

¼ cup orange liqueur

fresh mint leaves, *or*
sprigs, for garnish

## Making the Glaze:

1. The glaze isn't difficult to make but it is time-consuming. I recommend making the glaze on a rainy day when you have nothing pressing to do. Covered and stored in a jar in the fridge, the glaze keeps for several weeks.

2. Carefully remove the zest from the oranges in long wide strips using a vegetable peeler. With a paring knife, be sure to remove any white pith—you don't want this to taste bitter! Cut the wide zest strips into julienne strips.

3. Fill a saucepan ¾ full with cold water. Add the zest and bring to a boil. Boil for 1 minute; then drain in a sieve.

4. Return the zest to the saucepan and fill the saucepan again ¾ full with cold water. Bring to a boil, reduce the heat, and simmer for 10 minutes.

5. Drain the zest again.

6. Add 4 cups of water, 3 cups of sugar, and the salt to the saucepan. Bring to a boil, stirring until the sugar is dissolved.

7. Add the zest. Gently simmer uncovered, stirring occasionally, until the zest is completely translucent and the syrup has thickened (about 15-20 minutes).

8. Add the orange liqueur.
9. Pour the syrup into a plastic or glass container. Cover and refrigerate until ready to use.

**Poaching the Pears:**

1. In a saucepan, make a simple syrup by mixing 4 cups of water and 4 cups of sugar together. Bring almost to a boil, and then simmer for 10 minutes.
2. Add the lemon juice.
3. Peel the pears with a vegetable peeler. Cut the pears in half lengthwise. Use a melon baller to scoop out the seeds.
4. Starting at the wide part of the pears, slice them about half-way down toward the stem ends 5 to 6 times, depending on the size of the pears. This will allow you to fan each pear for a great presentation.
5. Using a slotted spoon, gently place the pear halves in the simple syrup, cut side up.
6. Simmer them until they are still somewhat firm but can be pierced with a tester, about 15 to 20 minutes.
7. Using the slotted spoon, place a pear half on each plate. Spoon a teaspoon of the glaze over the pear. Place several zest strips over top. Garnish with a sprig of mint.
8. Notes: The pears can be served hot, at room temperature, or cold. I recommend hot because the pears can turn brown quickly.
9. If you really want to be decadent, add a scoop of ice cream or crème fraîche just as you serve the fruit.

Sheer heaven!

# Cranberry-Raspberry Poached Pears

YVONNE MARTIN

*6 servings*

*Prep Time: 20 minutes* ❧ *Cooking Time: 15 to 30 minutes*

4 cups raspberry *or*
cranberry juice, *or*
2 cups raspberry and
2 cups cranberry juice

1 cup red wine
(The alcohol cooks off,
but if you prefer not to
use it, add 1 more cup
fruit juice instead.)

2 cups water

1 cup sugar

1 teaspoon cinnamon

1 teaspoon ginger

1 teaspoon whole cloves

6 whole pears

1. Put the juice, wine, water, sugar, cinnamon, ginger and cloves into a deep skillet or large saucepan. Bring to a simmer.
2. Meanwhile, prepare the pears by cutting them in half lengthwise. With a teaspoon, scoop the core out of each half.
3. Submerge the halves, cut side down in the hot liquid. If the liquid doesn't completely cover them, add more juice and water until it does.
4. Simmer 15 to 30 minutes until the pears become as soft as you like them. That will depend partly on how ripe they are. I test the pears with a toothpick or thin skewer.

**Notes:** *You can serve the pears hot, warm, or cold.*

*You can refrigerate the leftover cooking liquid for up to a week (in a tightly covered container) and re-use it. Simply refresh it with a little more wine, juice, and sugar.*

Use any type of pear that you want, and any kind of red fruit juice. We've made this recipe with cranberry, cranberry raspberry, and even cranberry pomegranate juices. Any one of these gives a lovely pink tint to the pears.

Poached pears topped with yogurt and granola make a lovely fruit starter for a breakfast or brunch. They can also be topped with a drizzle of chocolate sauce and whipped cream to make an elegant, gluten-free dessert for lunch or dinner.

# Mango Tango

ELLEN GUTMAN CHENAUX

*Serves 8*

*Prep Time: 10 minutes* ❧ *Chilling Time: 1 to 4 hours, until chilled through*

¼ seedless watermelon

2 mangoes, ripe, but not mushy

2 limes, juiced

zest of 2 limes

mint sprigs, for garnish

1. Cut the watermelon into bite-size chunks or use a melon baller to make watermelon balls. Transfer the watermelon pieces to a medium bowl.
2. Cut off the bottom of the mangoes so they will stand up straight. Use a sharp paring knife to remove the peel. Cut the mangoes into bite-size pieces. Add to the watermelon.
3. Use a microplane to grate the zest from the limes. Cover the zest and set it aside. Add the lime juice to the fruit and toss. Cover and refrigerate.
4. Remove the fruit from the refrigerator 15 minutes before serving.
5. Serve the fruit in martini glasses or parfait dishes. Sprinkle each serving lightly with the lime zest. Add a sprig of mint and serve.

*It takes two to tango, and combining these flavors will make you want to get up and dance!*

# Pineapple Napoleon

LYNNETTE SCOFIELD

*Serves 8*
*Prep Time: 30 minutes*

1 large ripe pineapple

8-ounce package cream cheese,
softened to room temperature

½ cup sour cream

4 tablespoons spoonable
pineapple ice cream topping,
such as Smuckers

¾ cup sifted confectioners sugar,
plus more for dusting on top

dash of salt

fresh berries for garnish

1. Remove the top of the pineapple and cut off the rind so that you form a square block.
2. Use an apple or pineapple corer to remove the tough center. Slice the pineapple block into thin square slices.
3. Mix the cream cheese, sour cream, ice cream topping, confectioners sugar, and salt. Stir until creamy.
4. Layer slices of pineapple alternating with the cream mixture. (Each serving should have 3 or 4 slices of pineapple.)
5. Top with fresh raspberries, strawberries, or your choice of berries, and a generous sprinkling of confectioners sugar.

**Notes:** *You can prepare the cream cheese filling the day before.*

*Use any leftover pineapple for fruit salad, or freeze it for a fruit smoothie.*

Just a touch of confectioners sugar and a sprig of mint makes this picture perfect.

Admit it, you want ice cream for breakfast, you know you do....so let's make it healthy with some lovely summer berries. The real surprise here is how hot baked pineapple and freezing cold ice cream can combine to make a wonderful morning fruit treat! What's wrong with having dessert for breakfast?

# Pineapple Sunrise

JOYCE SCHULTE

*Serves 8 (individual serving size: a ½- to 1-inch-thick slice)*
*Prep Time: 20 minutes    Baking Time: 30 to 40 minutes*

fresh pineapple, large
enough to cut into
8 round slices, each
½- to 1-inch thick

½ cup brown sugar

1 quart coconut, *or*
pineapple coconut,
ice cream

sprig of mint, *optional*

fresh assorted berries
(blueberries, raspberries,
blackberries, and/or
sliced strawberries)

toasted coconut, *optional*

1. Preheat the oven to 400°.
2. Grease the glass baking dish(es).
3. Peel and core the pineapple. Slice into 8 ½- to 1-inch-thick slices.
4. Place the pineapple slices in the glass baking dish(es). Sprinkle with brown sugar. (You can layer the pineapple. Just be sure to sprinkle each layer with brown sugar.)
5. Bake 30 to 40 minutes, or until the slices are soft. Note: You can do this the night before serving. If you do that, cover and refrigerate the pineapple till the morning. Pull out and reheat in the oven.
6. Place a slice of hot pineapple on each individual plate. Place a small scoop of coconut ice cream in the center of each slice. Top with a sprig of mint if you wish. Scatter fresh berries over the plate and pineapple. Sprinkle with toasted coconut, if you want.

# Grilled Watermelon Topped with Mango Salsa and Crème Fraîche

KRISTIE ROSSET

*Serves 6*
*Prep Time: 30 minutes* ❧ *Grilling Time: 5 minutes*

a good-sized watermelon

⅓ cup diced cantaloupe

⅓ cup diced watermelon

⅓ cup diced mango

1 tablespoon finely chopped fresh mint

1 cup, or so, crème fraîche

6 mint sprigs

1. Slice a full watermelon into 1½ inch rounds, then cut each into wedges, using 6 wedges for this recipe. (Reserve ⅓ cup diced watermelon.)
2. In a medium-sized bowl, make a fruit salsa by combining the diced watermelon, cantaloupe, mango, and chopped mint. Set aside.
3. Preheat your grill, either outdoors or a stove-top one. The grill should be very hot to achieve a quick sear. You do not want to cook the watermelon.
4. Sear each watermelon wedge on one side, and turn it over. Quickly sear the second side, then remove it promptly from the grill. Refrigerate the seared watermelon until ready to serve.
5. To serve, set one seared wedge on a dessert-sized plate and top with a large spoonful of mango salsa, a dollop of crème fraîche, and a mint sprig.

*Watermelon is a Southern staple in the summertime, and watermelon seed-spitting contests abound.*

As a child growing up in Arkansas, I was enthralled with seeing watermelon plants growing in what seemed like only days after spitting seeds in the yard!

At our Hot Springs, Arkansas, inn delicious summer breakfast appetizers include a melon and mint compote, watermelon wedges, and now we've added a striking new twist. Grilling the watermelon enhances its flavor and adds a hint of smoky goodness.

The key to grilling the watermelon successfully is to sear each side quickly over high heat. If the watermelon is cooked too slowly and heats the interior of the watermelon slice, you'll end up with a shrunken slice of mushy watermelon. This is bad! But a quickly seared watermelon is beautiful and ever-so tasty.

# Stewed Plums

DANIELLE HANSCOM

*Serves 4*
*Prep Time: 15 minutes    Cooking Time: 20 minutes*
*Chilling Time: 8 hours, or overnight*

6 large, ripe, red Italian
plums, washed

¼ cup water

½ cup pure maple syrup
(we like grade B for the flavor)

1 teaspoon ground cinnamon

1. Pit each plum and cut it into eighths.
2. Place plum pieces in a 2-quart saucepan.
3. Stir in water, maple syrup, and cinnamon.
4. Gently simmer for 15 to 20 minutes, depending on how firm the plums are, until tender but still holding their shape.
5. Remove from heat and let cool completely.
6. Cover with plastic wrap and refrigerate overnight.

**Note:** *For breakfast, serve these over plain Greek yogurt with a sprinkle of granola.*
*For dessert, serve them over vanilla ice cream.*

I think the plum is an overlooked fruit, and I always grab a big bag of them when they finally show up at the fruit stands. They make great tarts, but this fruit is also wonderful for breakfast or over ice cream. Heck, why not for breakfast over ice cream!

# Grilled Peaches or Nectarines

ELLEN GUTMAN CHENAUX

*Serves 4*

*Prep Time: 5 minutes*  ❦  *Grilling Time: 6 to 10 minutes*

2 ripe but firm peaches
*or* nectarines

berries *or* berry syrup

sorbet of your choice

mint leaf, for garnish

1. Preheat your grill to medium-high.
2. Slice the fruit in half and remove the pits.
3. Grease a barbecue basket or grill pan with cooking spray. Lay on the fruit, pit-side down.
4. Place the basket or grill pan on the grill and close the lid.
5. Grill the fruit for 5 to 8 minutes, until the fruit is warm, and there are grill marks on their tops.
6. Turn the basket over, or flip the fruit halves with tongs, close the grill lid, and cook for another minute or two.
7. Serve warm or at room temperature, filled with berries or a berry syrup.
8. Just before serving, top with a scoop of tangy sorbet and a mint leaf.

*Nothing says summer louder than the aroma of fresh peaches, and grilling them only adds to their heavenly scent. Add the berry filling as icing on the cake, so to speak.*

# Spiced Peach Compote

JOYCE SCHULTE

*Serves 14 to 15 (⅔ cup per person)*
*Prep Time: 4 minutes    Cooking Time: 20 to 25 minutes*
*Chilling Time: 8 hours*

5-pound bag fresh frozen peaches (peaches only; no sugar added)

1 cup water

1 cup sugar, *divided*

2 teaspoons apple pie spice (2 parts cinnamon, 2 parts nutmeg, 1 part allspice)

½ teaspoon ground ginger

fresh raspberries, *optional*

dried cranberries, *optional*

1. Put frozen peaches and water in a pot on the stove over medium heat.
2. As the peaches thaw and syrup begins to form, stir in ½ cup of sugar.
3. When more syrup forms and the peaches separate, stir in the remaining sugar, the apple pie spice, and the ginger.
4. Cook until the peaches are tender, stirring frequently.
5. Cool for one hour. After cooling, cover and place in the refrigerator.
6. The next morning, warm up the peaches on the stove, spoon into individual dishes, and top with fresh raspberries (if they're in season), or dried cranberries (for a great any-time fruit dish).

**Notes:** *Don't overcook the peaches. Don't use peaches frozen with sugar; that makes a too-sweet dish. Do make your own apple pie spice; it's just better.*

*For the best flavor, prepare this the night before for serving in the morning.*

A regular on the menu during the winter months at our inn, this warm compote, made with fresh frozen peaches, has been a favorite. Whether you eat it as a fruit dish, or put a little on top of your favorite oatmeal for a taste of summer in the morning, or have it as an evening dessert, it's a great way to enjoy the freshness of peaches in the middle of winter. Of course you can make it in the summer with fresh local peaches, too!

# Chilled Peach Soup

LYNNETTE SCOFIELD

*Serves 8*
*Prep Time: 30 minutes* ✿ *Chilling Time: 2 hours, or longer*

4 cups peeled and sliced fresh peaches, *or* frozen peaches that have been thawed

1 cup sour cream *or* vanilla yogurt, plus more for garnishing

8 ounces peach nectar

sugar, *optional*

dash of cinnamon

dash of salt

fresh mint leaves

1. In a large sturdy bowl, add sour cream or yogurt to the peaches. With an immersion or regular blender, blend until smooth.
2. Add peach nectar to the puréed peach mixture, and a bit of sugar, to taste, if you wish.
3. Add just a dash of cinnamon and a dash of salt.
4. Chill until cold throughout.
5. Serve in martini glasses with a drizzle of yogurt over the top and fresh mint leaves, whole or torn.

*Fresh peaches are always the best, but frozen will do nicely when peaches aren't in season.*

# Ray's Strawberry Soup

KRISTIE ROSSET

*Serves 8*

*Prep Time: 10 to 15 minutes* ❧ *Chilling Time: 2 to 4 hours*

1 quart strawberries, hulled and halved

4 cups low-fat buttermilk, *divided*

¾ cup sugar

⅔ cup sour cream

3 tablespoons peach schnapps *or* apple juice

fresh mint sprigs

1. Process the strawberries, 1 cup of buttermilk, and the sugar in a food processor. Set aside.
2. Combine the remaining 3 cups of buttermilk, sour cream, and peach schnapps or apple juice in a large bowl.
3. Pour the strawberry mixture into the sour cream mixture. Stir to combine. Cover and chill.
4. Serve chilled and garnished with mint sprigs.

We began serving Strawberry Soup during the very first summer that we opened the inn. It was a smashing hit, often requested, and is so easy to make. Refreshing and light on a hot summer morning!

# Blueberry/Blackberry Yogurt Parfait

DANIELLE HANSCOM

*Serves 4*
*Prep Time: 15 minutes (if not making the granola)*

12 ounces fresh blueberries *or* blackberries, rinsed

4 tablespoons agave syrup, *divided*

1 cup fat-free Greek yogurt

1 small ripe, but firm, banana, quartered lengthwise and cut into ½-inch pieces

½ teaspoon freshly grated lemon zest (from less than half a lemon)

½ cup granola (see recipe on page 208)

1. In a medium bowl, mix the berries and 2 tablespoons of agave syrup. Set aside.
2. In another medium bowl, mix the yogurt, banana, remaining 2 tablespoons of agave syrup, and lemon zest. Refrigerate for 10 minutes.
3. Starting with the berries, measure ¼ cup into each of 4 wine glasses.
4. Top each with a dollop of the yogurt mixture.
5. Repeat the layering one more time.
6. Refrigerate until ready to serve.
7. Sprinkle each parfait with granola just before serving.

This is a quick breakfast option for a breakfast-on-the-go. The yogurt topped with blackberries or blueberries can be added to a Mason jar, covered, and refrigerated overnight. Pack the granola separately to use later.

# Birchermuesli

DEBBIE MOSIMANN

*Serves 12*
*Prep Time: 15 minutes*

1 cup uncooked rolled oats

1½ cups plain, low-fat yogurt

1 large apple, peeled *or* unpeeled, and grated

1 large peach, peeled and sliced

½ cup red grapes, halved

6-ounce can mandarin oranges, with their juice

6-ounce can pineapple tidbits, with their juice

1 cup strawberries, quartered

½ cup walnuts, roughly chopped

¼ cup golden raisins

2 tablespoons lemon juice

1 teaspoon vanilla

1 tablespoon honey, or more or less

1. In a large bowl, combine all ingredients.
2. Mix just until blended, and serve immediately.

Birchermuesli may be one of the very first "health foods." Early in the 1900s, a Swiss doctor by the name of Max Bircher, advocated a raw diet as a form of healing. The centerpiece of that diet was Birchermuesli, a combination of fruits, oats, nuts, and yogurt. Today it is beloved by the Swiss, featured on many menus, and made as many different ways as there are Swiss cooks. Common to all are grated apples, oats and yogurt.

# Muffins, Scones, and Breads

## Batter Up

# Applesauce Date Muffins

YVONNE MARTIN

*Makes 36 muffins*
*Prep Time: 15 minutes ❧ Baking Time: 15 to 20 minutes*

3 cups chopped dates

2 teaspoons baking soda

1½ cups boiling water

6 cups flour

3 tablespoons baking powder

1½ teaspoons salt

1 tablespoon cinnamon

4 eggs

2½ cups brown sugar, lightly packed

1½ cups applesauce

1 cup vegetable oil

**Note:** *This recipe can be halved. Or make the full batch of batter and store whatever you don't need immediately in the fridge for up to two weeks.*

1. Preheat the oven to 375°.
2. Mix the chopped dates and baking soda together in a medium-sized bowl. Pour boiling water over top. Stir and then let stand.
3. In a large bowl, mix the flour, baking powder, salt, and cinnamon together.
4. In another good-sized bowl, beat the eggs with brown sugar. Beat in the applesauce and vegetable oil. Then mix in the date mixture.
5. Gently fold the liquid ingredients into the dry ingredients.
6. Spoon the batter into greased or paper-lined muffin tins, making them ¾ full.
7. Bake for 15 to 20 minutes, or until the muffin tops bounce back when you touch them lightly with your finger.
8. Let the muffins stand in the pan for about 5 minutes before removing them.

Before I owned an inn, I had several muffin recipes that allowed me to save the batter in the refrigerator for up to two weeks. All I had to do was simply scoop and bake in the morning to enjoy fresh, hot muffins any day of the week. This is one of my favorite muffin recipes.

# Apricot Walnut Muffins

YVONNE MARTIN

*Makes 12 Muffins*
*Prep Time: 15 minutes* ❧ *Baking Time: 15 to 18 minutes*

2 cups flour

1 cup quick-cooking oats

½ cup brown sugar,
lightly packed

1 tablespoon baking powder

2 teaspoons cinnamon

½ teaspoon salt

2 large eggs

1 cup milk

¼ cup vegetable oil

½ cup chopped apricots,
canned *or* fresh

½ cup chopped walnuts

1. Preheat the oven to 375°. Grease a 12-muffin baking tin.
2. Measure the flour, oats, brown sugar, baking powder, cinnamon, and salt into a large bowl. Mix together thoroughly. Make a well in the center.
3. In a separate bowl, beat the eggs, milk, and oil together.
4. Pour the wet ingredients into the well in the bowl of dry ingredients. Add the apricots and walnuts.
5. Using a spatula or wooden spoon, fold the dry ingredients into the wet ingredients just until they're combined.
6. Fill the greased muffin tins about ¾ full.
7. Bake for 15 to 18 minutes, or until the muffins are golden brown and firm to the touch.
8. Let the muffins stand in the pan for about 5 minutes before removing them.

This is a versatile recipe where you can take the basic recipe and add whatever dried fruits and nuts you have on hand. We like it with dried cherries and chopped almonds, or with craisins and pecans, too.

# Blueberry Buttermilk Muffins with Streusel Topping

JOYCE SCHULTE

*Makes 12 muffins*
*Prep Time: 20 minutes   Baking Time: 20 minutes*
*Cooling Time: 60 minutes*

**For the Muffins:**

¾ stick (6 tablespoons) butter, softened *or* melted

⅔ cup sugar

2 eggs

1 cup buttermilk

2 teaspoons vanilla

2¼ cups flour

½ teaspoon salt

1 teaspoon baking soda

2 teaspoons baking powder

½ teaspoon nutmeg

1½ cups frozen blueberries

1. Preheat the oven to 400°. Grease a 12-cup muffin baking tin.
2. Cream the butter and sugar until light and fluffy.
3. Add the eggs, buttermilk, and vanilla to the creamed mixture. Beat lightly until blended.
4. In another bowl, stir the flour, salt, baking soda, baking powder, and nutmeg together.
5. Add the dry mixture to the liquid ingredients. Stir just until the flour disappears.
6. Gently stir the blueberries into the batter.
7. Fill the muffin cups to the top. Bake for 20 minutes.
8. Let cool for 1 hour before removing muffins from the tin.

Once upon a time, in my early days as an innkeeper, I found a little cookbook shaped like a muffin. Its recipes became the backbone of all the muffins we served at our inn. We changed the recipes as we made them and made them our own, but it all started with the little muffin-shaped cookbook!

# Your choice of Streusel Toppings:

ELLEN GUTMAN CHENAUX

### Topping #1 Ingredients

1 cup brown sugar

1 cup all-purpose flour

1 stick (¼ pound) butter, very
cold and cut into chunks

1 cup rolled oats

fresh nutmeg

### Topping #1 Instructions

1. Combine the brown sugar, flour, and butter in a food processor. Pulse until the mixture is just combined.
2. In a medium-sized bowl, toss the mixture with the oats until combined.
3. Crumble over muffin, crisp, or cake batters just before baking. Grate the nutmeg on top.

### Topping #2 Ingredients

½ cup chopped walnuts

½ cup brown sugar

1½ teaspoons cinnamon

### Topping #2 Instructions

1. Mix the streusel topping ingredients in a bowl.
2. Sprinkle the streusel on top of the batter just before baking.

**Note:** *If you have any topping left over, put it in a plastic freezer bag and freeze it for future use. Streusels add a delicious crunch to muffins, coffee cakes, and fruit crisps. Keep a few batches in the freezer. Then they're always ready when you need them.*

# Upside-Down Sour Cherry Muffins

DEBBIE MOSIMANN

*Makes 10 muffins*
*Prep Time: 20 minutes ❧ Baking Time: 20 minutes*

2 cups frozen sour cherries, thawed and drained (the darker red, the better)

½ cup sugar

half a stick (¼ cup) melted butter

1½ cups flour

1½ teaspoons baking powder

⅛ teaspoon salt

½ cup sugar

1 egg

¾ cup milk

half a stick (¼ cup) melted butter

1 teaspoon vanilla

1. Preheat your oven to 375°. Spray 10 muffin cups with nonstick cooking spray.
2. Mix the cherries, ½ cup sugar, and half a stick of melted butter together well. Using a tablespoon, divide the cherry mixture among the 10 muffin cups.
3. In a good-sized bowl, mix the flour, baking powder, salt, and ½ cup sugar together.
4. Mix the egg, milk, and the other half stick of melted butter together in a separate bowl. Add these wet ingredients all at once to the dry ingredients.
5. Gently stir into a batter. Spoon the batter over the cherries in the muffin tins. (They'll be nearly full.)
6. Bake for 20 minutes, or until the cake part of the muffins bounces back when touched.
7. Remove from the oven. Run a knife around each muffin to loosen them.
8. Place a cookie sheet on top of the muffins. Then grasp the sides of the muffin tin and in one quick motion, turn the whole thing over, being careful to turn it away from yourself.
9. Allow to rest several seconds so the muffins loosen. Then gently raise the muffin tin, allowing little upside-down muffins to fall out.

Sour cherries are in season for such a short time, so I make sure to pit a bunch and freeze them so I can make these muffins in the winter, too. Bright and tart, these are a perennial favorite.

# Pomegranate Ginger Muffins

ELLEN GUTMAN CHENAUX

*Makes 12 muffins*
*Prep Time: 10 minutes*  *Baking Time: 15 to 20 minutes*
*Cooling Time: 5 to 10 minutes*

2 cups flour

⅔ cup sugar

1 tablespoon baking powder

½ teaspoon salt

⅓ cup crystallized ginger, minced

1 teaspoon lemon zest

1¼ cups pomegranate seeds

1 cup milk

1 egg, beaten

half a stick (¼ cup) butter, melted

sugar for topping

1. Preheat your oven to 425°. Grease a 12-cup muffin baking tin with cooking spray.
2. Mix the flour, sugar, baking powder, and salt in a large bowl.
3. Mix the ginger, lemon zest, pomegranate seeds, milk, egg, and melted butter in a medium-sized bowl.
4. Make a well in the dry ingredients. Pour the wet ingredients into the well. Stir until just mixed.
5. Spoon the batter into the muffin cups, making them ¾ full. Sprinkle the muffin tops with sugar.
6. Bake for 15 to 20 minutes, or until the muffins are puffed and golden, and a tester inserted into their centers comes out clean.
7. Let the muffins cool in the baking tin for 5 to 10 minutes. Remove the muffins from the pan and serve.

With the first bite, the
pomegranates explode in your
mouth, enhanced by their
pairing with crystallized
ginger for zing!

Christmas is a great time for
these festive muffins.
But why wait until Christmas?

# Strawberry Cornmeal Muffins

KATHRYN WHITE

*Makes 12 muffins*
*Prep Time: 12 to 15 minutes* ❧ *Baking Time: 20 to 25 minutes*

1 cup cornmeal

1 cup flour

⅓ cup sugar

2½ teaspoons baking powder

¼ teaspoon salt

2 cups strawberries, cut in small pieces

1 cup vanilla yogurt

¼ cup vegetable oil (canola is especially good)

1 egg, slightly beaten

1. Preheat your oven to 350°. Grease a 12-cup baking muffin pan, or line it with paper muffin cups.
2. In a large bowl, whisk together the cornmeal, flour, sugar, baking powder, and salt.
3. Add the diced strawberries. Toss gently to coat them with the flour mixture.
4. In a small bowl, whisk together the yogurt, oil, and egg.
5. Add the yogurt mixture to the flour mixture. Stir together until just combined. Do not over-mix.
6. Fill the muffin cups about ⅔ full. Bake 20 to 25 minutes or until a tester inserted into the centers of the muffins comes out clean.

When sweet, juicy strawberries are in season, these muffins are winners. The cornmeal adds a little something different to your morning muffin.

# Oat Bran Muffin Mix

YVONNE MARTIN

*Makes 4 batches of 12 muffins each*
*Prep Time for a batch of muffins: 20 minutes*
*Standing Time for a batch of muffins: 15 minutes*
*Baking Time for a batch of muffins: 20 minutes*

**For the Dry Mix:**

4 cups oat bran

3 cups dry oats

6 cups flour

2½ cups brown sugar, lightly packed

5 tablespoons baking powder

2 teaspoons salt

2 tablespoons cinnamon

*Mix all together and store in a large container.*

**For 1 batch of 12 Muffins**

2 cups milk

2 eggs

¾ cup vegetable oil

4 cups dry mix

1 cup chopped nuts

1½ to 2 cups dried fruit (I like apricots, craisins, and raisins)

1. About 15 to 30 minutes before you want to make the muffins, mix up the batter. Don't worry if it seems runny. The mixture will absorb the liquid both as it sits and as it bakes. You may need to add even more milk if it sits longer and thickens up.
2. Preheat your oven to 350°. Grease a 12-cup muffin baking tin to bake one batch.
3. Beat the milk, eggs, and vegetable oil together in a bowl. Set aside.
4. Place the dry mix ingredients in a large bowl. Pour in the wet ingredients. Add the nuts and dried fruit. Mix just until combined.
5. Let stand for at least 15 minutes.
6. Fill the greased muffin tins ¾ full.
7. Bake for about 20 minutes, or until a tester inserted into the center of the muffins comes out clean.
8. Let the muffins cool for 10 minutes before removing them from the baking tin.

**Note:** *Unused batter can be stored in the refrigerator for up to a week. You will need to add more milk before using it.*

# Oatmeal Granola Muffins

LYNNETTE SCOFIELD

*Makes 12 muffins*
*Prep Time: 30 minutes* ❧ *Baking Time: 20 minutes*

1 cup flour

1 cup quick oats

¾ cup granola

½ cup sugar

1 tablespoon baking powder

1½ teaspoons cinnamon

1 teaspoon salt

½ cup raisins (dried cranberries, apricots, cherries, *or* other dried fruit also work)

1 egg

1 cup water

¼ cup vegetable oil

1. Preheat the oven to 400°. Grease a 12-cup muffin baking tin or use paper liners.
2. In a large bowl, whisk together the flour, oats, granola, sugar, baking powder, cinnamon, and salt. Add raisins and stir them in with a rubber spatula or large spoon.
3. In a separate bowl, mix the egg, water, and oil with a whisk.
4. Pour the wet ingredients over the flour mixture. Stir just until moist. Do not over-stir.
5. Fill the muffin cups ¾ full.
6. Bake for 20 minutes for large muffins, or 14 to 15 minutes for mini-muffins, or until a tester inserted into the center of the muffins comes out clean.

*The beauty of these muffins is the variety you'll have by changing the additions of dried cranberries or apricots or ... whatever your imagination comes up with!*

# Shoofly Pie Muffins

DEBBIE MOSIMANN

*Makes 12 muffins*
*Prep Time: 15 minutes* ❧ *Baking Time: 40 to 45 minutes*

2 cups flour

1 cup brown sugar, lightly packed

1 stick (½ cup) butter *or* shortening, at room temperature

1 cup boiling water

½ cup baking molasses

1 teaspoon baking soda

¼ teaspoon salt

½ teaspoon vanilla

½ teaspoon cinnamon

1. Preheat your oven to 350°.
2. Mix together the flour and brown sugar in a good-sized mixing bowl. Cut in the butter or shortening, using two knives or a pastry cutter, until pea-sized crumbs form.
3. Set aside 1 cup of these crumbs to put on the tops of the muffins before baking.
4. Stir boiling water, molasses, and baking soda into the flour/brown sugar/butter crumbs (except those you're reserving to top the muffins).
5. Add salt, vanilla, and cinnamon to the mixture.
6. Line 12 muffin cups with muffin papers. Fill with batter.
7. Sprinkle the dry crumbs over top of the batter.
8. Bake for 40 to 45 minutes, or until a toothpick inserted into the center of the muffins comes out clean.

Pennsylvania Dutch Country, where we're located, is known for shoofly pie, a sweet pie made from molasses and brown sugar with mild spices. I have taken my love for this dessert and reworked those flavors and textures into this moist muffin that reaps praise every time I serve it.

# White Chocolate and Cranberry Tea Scones

YVONNE MARTIN

*Makes about 12 to 14 scones*
*Prep Time: 25 minutes* ❧ *Baking Time: 10 to 12 minutes*

2 cups flour

2 tablespoons sugar

4 teaspoons baking powder

½ teaspoon salt

5½ tablespoons (⅓ cup) butter, cut in chunks

2 eggs

½ cup half-and-half, *or* heavy cream

½ cup white chocolate chips

½ cup dried cranberries

1. Preheat your oven to 425°.
2. Mix together the flour, sugar, baking powder, and salt in a large bowl.
3. Cut in the butter, using either the pulse setting on a food processor, or by hand with a pastry blender. The mixture should resemble coarse crumbs, with no visible chunks of butter.
4. Separate one egg, setting the white aside in a small bowl. In a medium-sized bowl, beat the yolk with the other whole egg and half-and-half.
5. Add the wet ingredients to the flour-butter mixture, along with the white chocolate chips and cranberries. Stir with a fork until barely mixed.
6. Turn the dough onto a floured board and knead gently, about 6 to 8 times. Roll or pat the dough out to ½-inch thickness. Cut it into rounds with a biscuit cutter.
7. Place the rounds on an ungreased baking sheet about an inch apart. Brush the tops with the reserved egg white.
8. Bake for 10 to 12 minutes, or until the tops are golden brown.

*I love scones. I'll eat them for breakfast, lunch, or dessert. I also love cranberry and white chocolate chip cookies, so I've combined two of my favorite things in this recipe.*

# Fig and Kumquat Scones

DEBBIE MOSIMANN

*Makes 10 large scones*
*Prep Time: 20 minutes  ✿  Baking Time: 15 to 18 minutes*

2 cups flour

3 tablespoons sugar

1 tablespoon baking powder

½ teaspoon salt

1 stick (½ cup) butter, cold, cut into pieces

½ cup coarsely chopped dried figs

½ cup chopped fresh kumquats, any seeds removed

½ cup half-and-half

2 eggs

1. Preheat your oven to 400°.
2. Measure the flour, sugar, baking powder, and salt into a large bowl.
3. Add the pieces of butter, cutting it into the dry ingredients with a pastry blender or two knives, or mix Steps 2 and 3 in a food processor. The end result should be pea-sized crumbs.
4. Add the chopped figs and kumquats and toss till the fruit is well distributed throughout.
5. In a bowl mix the half-and-half and eggs. Reserve 2 tablespoons to brush on the tops of the scones.
6. Pour the wet ingredients into the flour-butter mixture. Using a fork, gently mix everything together just until you can pull it together into a cohesive dough.
7. Using an ice cream dipper, dip the dough onto a baking sheet lined with parchment paper, making 10 scones.
8. Brush the tops with the reserved egg mixture.
9. Bake for 15 to 18 minutes until browned and a toothpick inserted into the centers of the scones comes out clean.
10. Serve warm.

Scones, those rich and tender breakfast rolls, can take on many flavors. The sweetness of dried figs opposite the tart punch of the kumquats works so well. You can find kumquats from November through March.

# Matthew's Buttermilk Biscuits

DANIELLE HANSCOM

*Makes 14 (2½-inch) biscuits*
*Prep Time: 30 minutes ❧ Baking Time: 15 to 20 minutes*

3½ cups flour (White Lily is the best!)

½ cup whole wheat flour

4 teaspoons baking powder

1 teaspoon baking soda

1 teaspoon salt

2 sticks (1 cup) cold, unsalted butter, cut into small pieces

1½ cups buttermilk

1 stick (½ cup) melted, unsalted butter

1. Preheat oven to 450°.
2. Combine the white flour, whole wheat flour, baking powder, baking soda, and salt in a large bowl. Whisk together.
3. Using a pastry cutter, cut in the cold butter lightly, until the mixture resembles peas.
4. Pour the buttermilk into the batter. Mix together quickly, just until it starts to stick together.
5. Spread a little flour on your work surface. Transfer the biscuit dough to the work surface. Knead the dough together 1 or 2 times, and then pat it together with your hands. Do not overwork it.
6. Roll out the dough to about ¾-inch thick. Cut it with a round biscuit cutter, or cut it into 14 squares.
7. Place individual pieces on a sheet pan lined with parchment paper. Brush the tops with melted butter.
8. Bake for about 15 to 20 minutes, or until the biscuits just start to brown. Serve them warm with butter and jam.

# Blueberry Coffee Cake

DANIELLE HANSCOM

*Serves 16*

*Prep Time: 30 minutes* ✶ *Baking Time: 55 to 65 minutes* ✶ *Cooling Time: 35 to 40 minutes*

**Crumb Topping Ingredients**

1 cup sugar

1 cup flour

1 teaspoon cinnamon

1 stick (8 tablespoons) butter, at room temperature

**Crumb Topping Instructions**

1. In a good-sized bowl, mix together the sugar, flour and cinnamon.
2. With a pastry cutter, mix in soft butter until you have a crumb mixture the size of peas.
3. Set aside til needed.

*Coffee cakes are perfect for a do-ahead breakfast. The blueberries in this one keep it moist and add great flavor. Make it the day before you want to serve it, and take the pressure off the morning routine.*

## Cake Ingredients

2 cups flour

1 teaspoon baking powder

1 teaspoon baking soda

½ teaspoon salt

1 stick (8 tablespoons) butter, at room temperature

1 cup sugar

2 large eggs, at room temperature

1 cup buttermilk, at room temperature

1 teaspoon pure vanilla extract

½ teaspoon lemon extract

3 cups fresh blueberries mixed with one tablespoon of flour (to prevent the berries from sinking to the bottom of the batter)

## Glaze Ingredients

½ cup confectioners sugar

½ teaspoon vanilla

1½ teaspoons milk

## Cake Instructions

1. Preheat the oven to 350°. Butter and flour a 10-cup bundt pan.
2. In a large bowl, prepare the cake by mixing the flour, baking powder, baking soda, and salt together. Set aside.
3. In the mixing bowl of a stand mixer, beat the butter and sugar on medium speed just until smooth.
4. Add one egg at a time, mixing well in between.
5. Add the buttermilk, vanilla and lemon extracts. Mix until well incorporated.
6. Add the dry ingredients to the egg/sugar batter. Fold them together gently. This is best done by hand with a rubber spatula. Don't overdo it!
7. Gently fold in the blueberries.
8. Pour the batter into the prepared bundt pan.
9. Sprinkle with the crumb topping.
10. Bake for 55 to 65 min. Check if the cake is fully baked by inserting a wooden toothpick into its center. If it comes out clean, the cake is done. If it doesn't, continue baking, checking every 5 minutes or so.
11. Remove the cake from the oven and let it cool for 20 minutes.
12. Gently remove the cake from the pan onto a large plate. Then immediately flip the cake from the plate onto a wire baking rack so that the crumb topping is up. Let it cool for 15 to 20 minutes.
13. While the cake is cooling, mix the glaze ingredients together until smooth.
14. Set the plate under the rack to catch any drips. Drizzle the cake with the glaze.
15. Serve the cake while it's still warm.

*Tip:* *When preparing to make a cake or muffins, have all your ingredients at room temperature. The finished cake or muffins will have a better texture and flavor!*

# Strawberry Rhubarb Coffee Cake

LYNNETTE SCOFIELD

*Serves 12*
*Prep Time: 30 minutes   Baking Time: 45 to 50 minutes*
*Cooling Time: 15 minutes*

Springtime sings of rhubarb and strawberries, flavors that go so very well together. This coffee cake has a beautiful layer of both in the middle and is moist and flavorful. The cake is always a big hit at breakfast.

**Note:** *This recipe makes a large coffee cake. It can easily be baked in 2 smaller pans— then you can freeze one for another time!*

5 cups chopped rhubarb

¼ cup water

5 cups quartered strawberries

zest and juice of 1 lemon

½ cup cornstarch

1½ cups sugar

3 cups flour

1 cup sugar

2 teaspoons baking powder

1 teaspoon salt

2 sticks (1 cup) butter, softened

1 cup buttermilk

2 large eggs

1 teaspoon vanilla

½ teaspoon almond extract

¾ cup sugar

½ cup flour

half a stick (¼ cup) butter, softened

sweetened Greek yogurt, *optional*

1. Cook the rhubarb in a saucepan with ¼ cup water until just tender.
2. Add the strawberries and 3 tablespoons lemon juice.
3. In a small bowl, combine the cornstarch and 1½ cups sugar.
4. Add to the strawberries and rhubarb in the saucepan. Mix to combine. Then bring just to a boil, stirring constantly until thickened. Set aside.
5. Spray a 9- x 13-inch baking pan with nonstick spray. Preheat the oven to 375°.
6. In a large bowl, combine the 3 cups flour, 1 cup sugar, baking powder, salt, and lemon zest.
7. Add 2 sticks of butter cut into chunks. With your hands, work the butter into the flour mixture until crumbly.
8. In a separate bowl, combine the buttermilk, eggs, vanilla, and almond extract.
9. Pour the wet ingredients into the crumbly dry ingredients. Stir until well combined.
10. Pour half the batter into the prepared baking pan.
11. Spread the strawberry-rhubarb mixture on top of the batter.
12. Spoon the remainder of the batter over top of the berry mixture, being careful not to pull up the fruit.
13. In a bowl, combine the ¾ cup sugar, ½ cup flour, and half stick of butter into crumbs. Sprinkle on top of the batter.
14. Bake for 45 to 50 minutes, or until a tester inserted into the center of the cake comes out clean. (If you're baking in two smaller pans, check to see if the cake is done after 35 minutes.)
15. Allow to cool before cutting into squares. Serve with sweetened Greek yogurt.

# Cranberry-Orange Bread

JOYCE SCHULTE

*Makes 1 loaf*
*Prep Time: 20 minutes ❧ Baking Time: 60 to 70 minutes ❧ Cooling Time: 1 hour*

¼ stick (2 tablespoons) butter, at room temperature

1 egg

1 cup sugar

¾ cup orange juice

¼ teaspoon orange extract

2 cups flour

1 teaspoon baking powder

½ teaspoon baking soda

½ teaspoon salt

2 cups whole fresh, *or* thawed frozen, cranberries

½ cup chopped walnuts

1. Preheat your oven to 350°. Grease a 5- x 9-inch loaf pan.
2. In a large bowl, combine the butter, egg, and sugar. Mix well.
3. Add the orange juice, orange extract, flour, baking powder, baking soda, and salt. Stir until just moistened.
4. Fold in the cranberries and nuts.
5. Bake in the prepared loaf pan for 60 to 70 minutes, or until a tester inserted into the center of the bread comes out clean.
6. Cool for at least one hour before slicing.

Who says cranberries are only a winter treat? Cranberries freeze really well and last a long time. Fresh or frozen ones are so much better to bake with than dried ones, and they have less sugar. I buy them in season and freeze them. They're a great year-round treat.

# Pear Pecan Cardamom Bread

ELLEN GUTMAN CHENAUX

*Serves 20 (makes 2 loaves)*
*Prep Time: 15 minutes ❧ Baking Time: 1 hour ❧ Cooling Time: 1 hour*

1 cup canola oil

2 cups sugar

3 eggs

1 cup sour cream

2½ cups chopped pears
(Bosc are especially
good), peeled or not

1 cup coarsely chopped pecans

½ teaspoon orange zest

2 teaspoons vanilla extract

3 cups flour

½ teaspoon salt

1 teaspoon baking soda

1 teaspoon cinnamon

½ teaspoon nutmeg

½ teaspoon cardamom

additional sugar and
nutmeg, *optional*

1. Preheat your oven to 350°.
2. In a large mixing bowl, combine the oil, sugar, eggs, and sour cream. Blend well.
3. Stir in the pears, pecans, orange zest, and vanilla extract.
4. In another bowl, combine the flour, salt, baking soda, cinnamon, nutmeg, and cardamom.
5. Stir the dry ingredients into the pear mixture until just combined.
6. Grease two 5- x 9-inch loaf pans with cooking spray. Divide the batter between the loaf pans. If you wish, add a sprinkle of sugar mixed with a little nutmeg on top.
7. Bake for 1 hour, or until a tester inserted into the center of the loaves comes out clean.
8. Cool the loaves for 10 minutes. Then remove from the pans and cool on a wire rack to room temperature before slicing to serve.

You'll have everyone guessing what the secret ingredient is that provides such a unique flavor. I'll bet they won't guess it's cardamom.

# Pumpkin Bread

JOYCE SCHULTE

*Makes 3 loaves*
*Prep Time: 20 minutes*  ❧  *Baking Time: 1 hour*  ❧  *Cooling time: 1 hour*

3 cups flour

3½ cups sugar

1½ teaspoons cinnamon

1½ teaspoons nutmeg

1½ teaspoons salt

2 teaspoons baking soda

1 cup vegetable oil (corn oil is especially good)

⅔ cup water

4 eggs

15-ounce can pumpkin, *or* slightly less than 2 cups home-prepared pumpkin

1½ cups chopped walnuts

**Note:** *These loaves freeze well.*

1. Preheat the oven to 350°. Grease and flour three 5- x 9-inch loaf pans.
2. Mix together the flour, sugar, cinnamon, nutmeg, salt, and baking soda in a large bowl.
3. Add the oil, water, eggs, and pumpkin. Mix with an electric mixer until well blended.
4. Stir in the chopped nuts.
5. Divide the batter among the loaf pans.
6. Bake for 1 hour, or until a tester inserted into the center of the loaves comes out clean.
7. Let the breads cool in their pans for 1 hour.

At our inn we had a rule: there must always be a loaf of pumpkin bread in the freezer! This was originally my mother's recipe, and while she always left out the nuts, I always add them, loving the walnut flavor with the pumpkin. If you needed an early breakfast to go from the Chambered Nautilus, it was almost guaranteed there would be a slice of pumpkin bread for you!

# Sunflower Pumpkin Bread

LYNNETTE SCOFIELD

*Makes 2 loaves*

*Prep Time: 20 minutes* ❧ *Baking Time: 55 minutes* ❧ *Cooling Time: 1 hour*

2½ cups flour

2 cups sugar

2 teaspoons baking soda

½ teaspoon cinnamon

½ teaspoon ginger

½ teaspoon allspice

½ teaspoon salt

1½ cups pumpkin

½ cup vegetable oil

½ cup sunflower seeds

½ cup finely chopped walnuts

2 cups dried cranberries, coarsely chopped

1. Preheat your oven to 350°. Grease and flour two 8½- x 4½- x 2½-inch loaf pans.
2. Place the flour, sugar, baking soda, cinnamon, ginger, allspice, and salt in a medium-sized bowl. Stir to combine.
3. Mix the pumpkin and vegetable oil in a large bowl.
4. Add the dry ingredients to the wet ingredients. Mix in the sunflower seeds, chopped walnuts, and dried cranberries. The batter will be stiff.
5. Divide the batter between the 2 prepared loaf pans.
6. Bake for 55 minutes, or until a toothpick inserted in the centers of loaves comes out clean.
7. Let the breads cool in their pans for 1 hour.

*This is one of our favorite breads and most requested recipes. The fact that it's vegan doesn't diminish its flavor or texture at all!*

# Melodious Poppy Seed Bread

KRISTIE ROSSET

*Makes 2 or 3 loaves*
*Prep Time: 25 minutes    Baking Time: 50 minutes*
*Cooling Time: 5 to 10 minutes between baking and glazing*

**For the Bread:**

3 cups flour

1½ teaspoons salt

1½ teaspoons baking powder

3 eggs

1½ tablespoons poppy seeds

1½ cups milk

1 cup oil

2½ cups sugar

1½ teaspoons vanilla

1½ teaspoons almond extract

1½ teaspoons butter extract

**For the Glaze:**

¼ cup orange juice

¾ cup sugar

½ teaspoon vanilla

½ teaspoon almond extract

½ teaspoon butter extract

1. Preheat your oven to 350°.
2. In a large bowl, mix all bread ingredients together well.
3. Pour into 2 *or* 3 greased 5- x 9-inch loaf pans.
4. Bake the loaves for approximately 50 minutes, until a tester inserted into the loaves' centers comes out clean.
5. Let the bread cool in their pans 5 to 10 minutes.
6. Mix together all glaze ingredients in a bowl.
7. Drizzle the glaze over the loaves while the bread is still in the pan and warm.
8. Let cool before slicing and serving.

This sweet bread has been in my family for decades. Originally, I received the recipe from my brother-in-law Deryl, residing in Lincoln, Nebraska. He's a funny and intelligent guy, and no slouch when it comes to Poppy Seed Bread. This bread pairs well with a savory breakfast entrée. Or just nibble at it while enjoying a cup of coffee.

# Honey Oat Bread

LYNNETTE SCOFIELD

*Makes 2 loaves*
*Prep Time: 30 minutes* ✻ *Rising Time: 1 hour and 20 minutes*
*Baking Time: 40 minutes*

1¾ cups warm water, *divided*

1 tablespoon dry yeast

¾ cup quick-cooking oats

⅔ cup honey

3 tablespoons vegetable oil

2½ teaspoons salt

about 5 cups flour

1 egg, beaten

additional quick-cooking oats

*This was the first homemade bread we ever made at the Inn, and it's still a hit. A touch of honey adds a delightful sweetness.*

1. Stir ¼ cup warm water and yeast together in a large bowl. Let stand for 10 minutes, or until the yeast is dissolved.
2. Stir in the remaining water, oats, honey, oil, and salt. Stir in enough flour to form a soft dough.
3. Coat another large bowl with oil. Transfer the dough to the oiled bowl and turn it to coat.
4. Cover the dough with plastic wrap and then a kitchen towel. Let the dough rise at room temperature until it doubles in volume, roughly 1 hour.
5. Oil two 5- x 7-inch loaf pans. Punch down the dough, and then shape it into 2 loaves. Place 1 loaf in each pan.
6. Cover the loaves. Let them rise in a warm, draft-free area until they almost double in volume, about 20 minutes.
7. Preheat oven to 350°.
8. Brush the tops of the loaves with beaten egg. Sprinkle additional oats on top.
9. Bake for about 40 minutes, or until the loaves are brown on top, and a tester inserted into their centers comes out clean.

# Cinnamon Buns

KATHRYN WHITE

*Makes 12 rolls*
*Prep Time: 25 to 30 minutes* ❧ *First Rising Time: 60 to 90 minutes*
*Second Rising Time: 40 minutes, or overnight in the fridge*
*Baking Time: 30 to 35 minutes*

## Dough Ingredients

2 tablespoons active dry yeast

¼ cup warm water (90°)

1 teaspoon sugar

⅔ cup warm whole milk (90°)

¾ stick (6 tablespoons) unsalted butter

4 tablespoons sugar

1 teaspoon salt

2 large eggs, lightly beaten

4 cups unbleached flour

## Dough Instructions

1. In a large bowl add the warm water to the yeast and 1 teaspoon of sugar. Stir until the yeast is dissolved. Let the mixture sit for a few minutes until it starts to bubble.
2. Pour the milk, butter, and 4 tablespoons of sugar into a saucepan over medium-low heat. As the butter melts, stir to combine the ingredients. When well mixed, remove the saucepan from the heat.
3. Place the salt and eggs in a small bowl or 4-cup measuring cup. Add the warm milk mixture and stir to combine.
4. Add the liquid to the yeast.
5. Stir in the flour one cup at a time. The dough will become stiffer as the flour is added. Remove the dough from the bowl when it becomes too stiff to stir, and place it on a well-floured surface to begin kneading.
6. Rinse the large bowl and butter it. The dough will rise in it when it's ready.
7. Knead the dough for about 5 to 7 minutes, adding flour as necessary to keep it from sticking to the work surface. The dough will become elastic and smooth.
8. Place the dough in the buttered bowl, cover it with a clean towel, and let it rise in a warm place for about 1½ hours. It may take longer depending on how warm your kitchen is.

## Filling Ingredients

half a stick
(4 tablespoons)
unsalted butter at
room temperature,
plus more for
greasing the
baking pan

½ cup brown sugar

2 teaspoons
cinnamon

½ teaspoon grated
fresh nutmeg

## Filling Instructions

1. Grease the bottom and sides of a 9- x 13-inch baking pan.
2. Roll the raised dough into an 18- x 12-inch rectangle.
3. Brush the 4 tablespoons of softened butter over the top of the dough.
4. Combine the brown sugar, cinnamon, and nutmeg in a small bowl. Sprinkle the mixture over the buttered dough.
5. Beginning with the 18-inch side, roll the dough up jelly-roll style.
6. Cut the roll into 12 even slices. Place each slice face down in the baking pan in rows of three. Cover and let the slices rise until nearly doubled (or refrigerate overnight; in the morning bring to room temperature before baking).
7. Bake at 350° for 30 to 35 minutes, or until the tops are nicely browned.
8. Remove from the oven and wait about 5 minutes before inverting the pan of buns onto a baking sheet.
9. Spread the Cream Cheese Frosting over the buns while they're still warm.

## Cream Cheese Frosting Ingredients

8-ounce package
cream cheese, at
room temperature

half a stick
(4 tablespoons)
unsalted butter, at
room temperature

2 cups confectioners
sugar

1 teaspoon vanilla

pinch of salt

## Cream Cheese Frosting Instructions

1. Using a handheld mixer, blend the cream cheese and butter until combined (about 30 seconds on medium speed).
2. Stir in the sugar and blend until the frosting is of a spreadable consistency.
3. Stir in the vanilla and salt.
4. Use a spatula or knife to ice the rolls.

Cinnamon buns are one of my favorite comfort foods. The aroma of cinnamon from the oven is heavenly. Be sure to enjoy them with a fresh cup of coffee and the morning news.

# Lemon Ginger Rolls

DEBBIE MOSIMANN

*Makes 18 rolls*
*Prep Time: 15 minutes* ❧ *First Rising Time: 1 hour*
*Shaping Time: 15 minutes* ❧ *Second Rising Time: 30 minutes, or overnight in the fridge*
*Baking Time: 30 minutes*

## Roll Ingredients

6 cups flour

1 packet, *or*
1 tablespoon, yeast

¼ cup sugar

1 tablespoon salt

zest of 1 lemon; reserve the lemon itself for the glaze

1 cup hot water

1 stick (8 tablespoons) butter, cut into chunks

1 cup milk

½ cup candied ginger, minced

1 egg, beaten

## Glaze Ingredients

zest of a second large lemon

1 cup confectioners sugar

## Roll Instructions

1. Mix the flour, yeast, sugar, salt, and lemon zest together in a large bowl.
2. Pour hot water into a good-sized bowl. Add the butter to the hot water, stirring it and allowing it to melt.
3. Stir the milk into the water and butter. Cool until just warm.
4. Add the liquids to the dry ingredients. In a stand mixer, use the dough hook to mix for 2 to 3 minutes, or until the dough appears smooth. If sticky, add flour little by little until it pulls away from the side of the bowl.
5. Add the minced candied ginger and knead for a minute longer.
6. Remove the bowl from the mixer, cover it, and place it in a warm, draft-free place until the dough doubles in size, about 1 hour.
7. Shape the dough into 2-inch balls. Place 9 on a baking sheet, without touching each other.
8. Cover with a light towel and allow the balls to double in size. This will take about 30 minutes in a warm, draft-free place. Or you can put them in the fridge overnight, covered, for a slow, cold rise.

9. When ready to bake, preheat the oven to 350°. (If you've had the rolls in the fridge overnight, take them out and let them reach room temperature, about 30-45 minutes.) Brush the tops of the rolls with beaten egg.

10. Bake for 30 minutes, or until golden brown. Remove from the oven and cool.

**Glaze Instructions**

11. Mix the lemon juice from the reserved lemon, zest from the second lemon, and confectioners sugar until smooth.

12. When the rolls are almost cool, glaze them.

13. Serve them with honey butter.

**Notes:** *By giving the rolls a second rising time in the refrigerator overnight, you can serve freshly baked yeast rolls for breakfast. This slow cold rise gives them a particularly fine texture. Allow the dough to warm a bit to room temperature before baking.*

I am a fan of all things lemon. Adding lemon and candied ginger to a slightly sweet yeast dough gives rolls a burst of brightness and flavor that turns them into something extraordinary.

# English Muffins

LYNNETTE SCOFIELD

*Makes 16 to 18 muffins*

*Prep time: 30 minutes* ❧ *Rising time: 30-45 minutes* ❧ *Griddle time: 10-12 minutes*

2 packages active dry yeast

2 cups warm water

5 to 6 cups flour, *divided*

1 tablespoon sugar

1 tablespoon salt

½ cup shortening, *or* vegetable oil

cornmeal for sprinkling

1. In a large bowl, dissolve the yeast in warm water.
2. Add 3 cups flour, the sugar, salt, and shortening to the yeast mixture, stirring by hand until smooth.
3. Gradually add the remaining 2 to 3 cups of flour to form a stiff dough.
4. On a floured surface, gently knead the dough 5 to 6 times until it's no longer sticky.
5. Roll the dough to ¼-inch thickness. Cut out the muffins with a round cutter.
6. Sprinkle cornmeal evenly over 2 ungreased baking sheets. Place the cut-out dough on the cornmeal. Sprinkle each muffin with additional cornmeal.
7. Cover the filled baking sheets loosely with plastic wrap and towels. Let rise for 30 to 45 minutes in a draft-free, warm place.
8. Heat an ungreased griddle to 350°. Place each muffin cut-out on the griddle without crowding them. (You'll need to do several batches, depending on the size of your griddle.)
9. Cook for 5 to 6 minutes on each side, or until golden brown.

These take a surprisingly short amount of time compared to what you would expect. They draw oohs and aahs, because they're so delicious—and how often do you get homemade ones?

# Have you tried these?

Kiss My Grits, Page 180

Omelet with Variations, page 124

Ginger Spice Pancakes, page 92

Glazed Bacon, page 186

# Sweet Breakfasts
## Guilty Pleasures

# Banana Sour Cream Pancakes

LYNNETTE SCOFIELD

*Serves 4 to 6*
*Prep Time: 10 minutes* ❧ *Griddle Time: 5 to 7 minutes for each griddle-full*

2 cups flour

2 teaspoons
baking powder

1 teaspoon baking soda

2 tablespoons sugar

½ teaspoon cinnamon

2 cups sour cream
*or* yogurt

2 eggs

⅓ cup oil

2 to 3 ripe bananas,
mashed

1. Preheat your griddle to 350°. Use oil or butter to grease the griddle.
2. In a medium-sized bowl, whisk together the flour, baking powder, baking soda, sugar, and cinnamon.
3. In a separate bowl, combine the sour cream, eggs, and oil.
4. Pour the liquid ingredients into the dry ones and mix until just combined.
5. Stir in the mashed bananas.
6. Place about ⅓ to ½ cup of the batter on the griddle for each pancake. Cook until the bottom of the pancake is golden brown and the bubbles on top pop and stay open.
7. Flip each pancake to finish cooking, about 2 to 3 minutes more.
8. Serve immediately.

*These pancakes prove that you can make something wonderful with well-ripened bananas other than banana bread!*

# Lemon Ricotta Pancakes

DANIELLE HANSCOM

*Serves 4 to 5 (makes about 14 [3½-inch] pancakes)*
*Prep Time: 15 minutes ⚭ Griddle Time: 8 minutes, per griddle-full*

¾ cup flour

1 teaspoon baking powder

4 tablespoons sugar

½ teaspoon salt

6 large eggs, separated

1½ cups ricotta cheese

¼ stick (2 tablespoons) unsalted butter, melted

2 tablespoons grated lemon zest (from 2 to 3 large lemons)

1. Preheat your griddle to medium hot.
2. In a medium-sized bowl, mix the flour, baking powder, sugar, and salt together. Set aside.
3. Separate the eggs. Set the whites aside.
4. Mix the yolks in a large bowl with the ricotta cheese, melted butter, and lemon zest.
5. Slowly and gently fold the dry ingredients into the egg-cheese mixture.
6. Whip the egg whites with an electric mixer until soft peaks form.
7. Carefully fold the beaten egg whites into the batter.
8. Spray the griddle with non-stick cooking spray.
9. Ladle a scant ½ cup of batter for each pancake onto the griddle. Cook until lightly browned on the bottom. Flip and repeat on the other side. Cook for approximately 4 minutes on each side. Keep an eye on them; different griddles cook at different speeds and heat.
10. Serve immediately with fresh strawberries or raspberries and Lemon Curd (recipe on page 220) on the side.

*The combination of lemon and ricotta in a pancake is simply divine.*

The cornmeal allows these pancakes to have a slight bit of crunch around the edges. Although the recipe suggests blending the blueberries into the mixture, you can also drop blueberries on top of the batter, just after placing the mixture on the griddle.

# Blueberry Cornmeal Pancakes

KATHRYN WHITE

*Makes 16 4-inch pancakes*
*Prep Time: 10 minutes* ❧ *Griddle Time: 5 to 7 minutes for each griddle-full*

2 cups flour, plus 1 tablespoon flour for coating the blueberries, *divided*

1 cup ground cornmeal

⅓ cup sugar

2 teaspoons baking powder

½ teaspoon baking soda

¾ teaspoon cinnamon

½ teaspoon salt

1 cup vanilla yogurt

1½ cups milk

4 large eggs

¾ stick (6 tablespoons) unsalted butter, melted

2 tablespoons grated orange zest

2 cups blueberries

1. In a large bowl, combine 2 cups of flour, cornmeal, sugar, baking powder, baking soda, cinnamon, and salt. Use a whisk to blend.
2. In separate smaller bowl, blend the yogurt, milk, eggs, melted butter, and orange zest.
3. Pour the liquid ingredients into the flour mixture and blend, being careful not to over-mix.
4. In a separate bowl, lightly coat the blueberries with the tablespoon of flour. Then stir the blueberries into the batter.
5. Preheat your griddle to 350°. Cook until the bottom of each pancake is golden brown and the bubbles on top pop and stay open.
6. Flip each pancake to finish cooking, about 2 to 3 minutes more.
7. Serve with warm syrup and your favorite bacon or sausage, if you wish.

# Blueberry Sour Cream Pancakes with Lemon Sauce

LYNNETTE SCOFIELD

*Serves 4 to 6*

*Prep Time: 10 minutes* ❧ *Cooking Time: 3 to 5 minutes for each griddle-full*

2 cups flour

2 teaspoons
baking powder

1 teaspoon baking soda

2 tablespoons sugar

2 eggs

2 cups sour cream,
*or* plain yogurt

⅓ cup oil

2 cups blueberries

1. Preheat your griddle. Use oil or butter to grease the griddle.
2. In a medium bowl, whisk together the flour, baking powder, baking soda, and sugar.
3. In a separate bowl, combine the eggs, sour cream, and oil.
4. Pour the sour cream mixture into the dry ingredients. Stir until just combined.
5. Drop about ½ cup batter onto the griddle for each pancake. Drop blueberries onto each pancake. Cook until the bottom of the pancake is golden brown and the bubbles on top pop and stay open.
6. Flip each pancake to finish cooking, for about 2 to 3 minutes.
7. Serve immediately with Lemon Sauce.

Who doesn't love blueberry pancakes?
These take those pancakes up one beautiful notch!

# Lemon Sauce

*Makes 1¼ cups sauce*

½ cup sugar

1 cup hot water

1½ tablespoons cornstarch

¼ stick (2 tablespoons) butter, cut into slices

1 tablespoon grated lemon zest

2 tablespoons lemon juice

1. In a medium saucepan, combine the sugar, hot water, and cornstarch. Stir until smooth.
2. Stir in the butter and lemon zest. Cook until the mixture thickens to a syrup consistency.
3. Stir in the lemon juice.

# Pumpkin-Ginger Pancakes

JOYCE SCHULTE

*Serves 4 (2 large pancakes each)*
*Prep Time: 10 minutes  ❧  Griddle Time: 6 to 8 minutes, per griddle-full*

## Pancakes Ingredients

1 cup flour

¼ teaspoon salt

2 tablespoons brown sugar

1 teaspoon baking powder

½ teaspoon baking soda

½ teaspoon cinnamon

½ teaspoon nutmeg

½ teaspoon powdered ginger

1 egg, beaten

½ cup plain yogurt

¾ cup milk

¾ cup canned pumpkin

¼ stick (2 tablespoons) melted butter

fresh pear slices

warm maple syrup

## Pancake Instructions

1. In a medium-sized bowl, sift together the flour, salt, brown sugar, baking powder, baking soda, cinnamon, nutmeg, and powdered ginger.
2. In a large bowl, combine the beaten egg, yogurt, milk, pumpkin, and melted butter.
3. Add the flour mixture to the wet ingredients. Stir until just blended.
4. Heat the pancake griddle and grease with butter. Use a scant ½ cup batter per pancake. Cook until the pancakes are lightly browned on the bottom.
5. Flip and repeat on the other side. Cook for approximately 4 minutes on each side.
6. Serve with gingered butter, fresh pear slices and warm maple syrup.

## Gingered Butter Ingredients

2 tablespoons finely chopped candied ginger

half a stick (¼ cup) softened butter

## Gingered Butter Instructions

1. Beat the ginger and butter together. This keeps well in the refrigerator.

Pumpkins are traditionally thought
of as a fall food, but at our inn
we've used pumpkin year-round and
this has been one of our favorites.
This recipe makes very moist pancakes
and when served with gingered butter
and topped with fresh pear slices,
they are simply delicious. Pumpkin
Pancakes + Pears = Fall at its best!

# Ginger Spice Pancakes

JOYCE SCHULTE

*Serves 6 (2 pancakes per person)*
*Prep Time: 20 minutes    Cooking Time: 10 minutes*

2½ cups flour

5 teaspoons baking powder

1½ teaspoons salt

1 teaspoon baking soda

1 teaspoon cinnamon

½ teaspoon ginger

¼ cup molasses

2 cups milk

2 eggs

¾ stick (6 tablespoons) butter, melted

1 cup raisins

confectioners sugar, for garnish

1. Preheat the griddle. Spray it with non-stick cooking spray, or brush it with oil or butter.
2. In a large bowl, combine the flour, baking powder, salt, baking soda, cinnamon, and ginger.
3. Add the molasses, milk, eggs, and melted butter. Beat together with an electric mixer until well blended.
4. Stir in the raisins.
5. Ladle about ½ cup of batter for each pancake onto the hot griddle. Turn the pancakes when their edges are dry and bubbles rise to the surface and hold there.
6. Sprinkle with confectioners sugar just before serving. Serve with Cinnamon Syrup.

One day we found a recipe for an amazing cinnamon syrup (see page 93), but what to put it on? We combined ingredients and ended up with ginger spice pancakes. Over the years this recipe evolved. We added the raisins, making it a rich winter pancake. A versatile recipe, the pancakes made from it even taste great plain!

# Cinnamon Syrup

JOYCE SCHULTE

*Makes 1½ cups*

*Cooking Time: 5 to 7 minutes ❧ Cooling Time: 30 minutes or more*

1 cup sugar

½ cup light corn syrup

¼ cup water

¼ teaspoon ground cinnamon (use a touch more for a stronger flavor)

½ cup whipping cream

1. In a small saucepan, stir together the sugar, corn syrup, water, and cinnamon.
2. Stirring constantly, bring the mixture to a boil over moderate heat. Boil for 2 minutes. Remove from heat.
3. Stir in the cream.
4. Cool for at least 30 minutes. The syrup will thicken as it cools.
5. Serve warm or at room temperature on pancakes, French toast, and waffles.
6. The syrup can be refrigerated for a week or two.

# Spice Pancakes with Lemon Sauce

KATHRYN WHITE

*Serves 4*

*Prep Time: 10 minutes*  *Griddle Time: 5 to 7 minutes per griddle-full*

2 large eggs

2½ cups buttermilk

¼ stick (2 tablespoons) melted butter

1 tablespoon sugar

2 teaspoons dark molasses

2 cups flour

½ cup oats, quick *or* regular

2 teaspoons baking powder

1 teaspoon baking soda

2 teaspoons ground ginger

1 teaspoon ground cinnamon

½ teaspoon ground nutmeg

¼ teaspoon ground cloves

pinch of salt

1. Separate the eggs. Beat the egg whites in a deep bowl on high speed until they hold moist peaks. Set them aside.
2. Beat the egg yolks in a large bowl with the buttermilk, melted butter, sugar, and molasses.
3. Add the flour, oats, baking powder, baking soda, ginger, cinnamon, nutmeg, cloves, and salt to the egg-yolk mixture. Beat until well mixed.
4. Gently fold the whipped egg whites into batter until just combined.
5. Preheat the griddle. Butter it. Pour enough batter onto the griddle to form pancakes that are 4 to 5 inches in diameter. Cook over medium heat until the tops are full of bubbles.
6. Flip the pancakes. Cook another 1 to 2 minutes until they're golden brown.
7. Serve with warm Lemon Sauce (page 219).

# Granola Pancakes

KRISTIE ROSSET

*Serves 6*
*Prep Time: 10 minutes ❧ Soaking Time: Overnight*
*Griddle Time: 5 to 7 minutes per griddle-full*

2 cups milk

1 cup granola

1 cup rolled oats

half a stick (¼ cup)
butter, melted

½ cup flour

2 large eggs, beaten

2 tablespoons sugar

2 teaspoons baking powder

¼ teaspoon nutmeg

¼ teaspoon cinnamon

¼ teaspoon salt

butter for griddle

1. The night before making granola pancakes, combine the milk, granola, and rolled oats. Cover and place in the refrigerator overnight.
2. In the morning, combine the melted butter, flour, beaten eggs, sugar, baking powder, nutmeg, cinnamon, and salt in a good-sized bowl.
3. Stir into the granola mixture. Combine just until smooth, but do not over-mix.
4. Preheat the griddle. Butter the griddle.
5. Using a ¼-cup measure for each pancake, pour the batter onto the hot buttered griddle.
6. Bake until bubbles appear on the surface, then flip and bake until done, about 2 to 3 minutes on the second side.
7. Serve warm with Lemon Brandied Apples (recipe on page 11).

*Soak the granola in these pancakes overnight, and you'll have pancakes with a moist yet chewy texture.*

# Whole Wheat Pancakes with Roasted Pecans

KRISTIE ROSSET

*Makes 12 pancakes*
*Prep Time: 30 minutes* ❧ *Griddle Time: 5 to 7 minutes per griddle-full*

¾ cup flour

¾ cup whole wheat flour

3 tablespoons sugar

1½ teaspoons baking powder

½ teaspoon baking soda

½ teaspoon salt

1½ cups buttermilk
(low-fat is fine)

1 tablespoon vegetable oil

1 large egg

1 large egg white, beaten

¾ cup maple syrup

½ cup chopped pecans, roasted

dollops of whipped cream

1. Lightly spoon flours into dry measuring cups. Level with a knife.
2. Combine flours, sugar, baking powder, baking soda, and salt in a large bowl, stirring with a whisk.
3. In a separate bowl, combine buttermilk, oil, and egg. Stir until well blended, then gently fold in beaten egg white.
4. Add liquid ingredients to flour mixture, stirring just until moistened.
5. Heat griddle over medium-low heat. Add a light coating of oil.
6. Spoon about ¼ cup batter per pancake onto griddle. Turn pancakes over when tops are covered with bubbles and edges look cooked.
7. Serve with maple syrup, roasted pecans, and a dollop of whipped cream.

**Note:** *These pancakes are thick, so be patient and do not try to cook them too fast!*

# Puff Pancakes

DANIELLE HANSCOM

*Serves 8*

*Prep Time: 10 minutes* ✿ *Chilling Time: 10 minutes*
*Baking Time: for small pancakes—15 minutes; for large pancakes—20 to 30 minutes*

4 large eggs, at room
temperature

1 cup half-and-half

1 cup flour

half a stick (¼ cup)
unsalted butter

**Sweet Toppings**

Fresh, slightly sweetened
berries of any kind; sliced
peaches; puréed peaches
with a bit of maple syrup; fried
bananas; warm applesauce;
sautéed apples; lemon juice;
toasted nuts—all sprinkled
with confectioners sugar

**Savory Toppings**

Chopped tomatoes with
pesto; wilted spinach
with a poached egg;
caramelized onion and
grated smoked Gouda

1. Preheat the oven to 450°.
2. In a large bowl, whisk together the eggs and half-and-half thoroughly.
3. Sift the flour over the egg mixture; then whisk until smooth. Refrigerate for 10 minutes.
4. Spray 8 ramekin dishes, or one 8- x 8-inch ovenproof baking dish with nonstick cooking spray.
5. Add ½ tablespoon butter to each ramekin dish (or 2 tablespoons to a large dish). Put the container(s) into the hot oven for 1 minutes to melt the butter. Be careful, the hot oven will burn the butter if you leave it in too long.
6. Be careful not to burn yourself when you do the next step because the oven will be very hot. It is best (if you can) to pull out the shelf holding the dish(es). Add all of the batter to the single baking dish, or approximately ⅓ cup to each ramekin dish. Then slide the shelf carefully back into the oven. Do this as quickly as possible to prevent the heat from escaping.
7. Bake the ramekins 10 to 15 minutes; the large dish 20 to 30 minutes. Finished pancakes will be puffed up with crispy and lightly browned edges.
8. Serve at once with a topping of your choice.

# Chocolate Chip Buttermilk Pancakes

JOYCE SCHULTE

*Serves 6 (2 pancakes per person)*
*Prep Time and Standing Time for the Strawberries: 20 minutes*
*Prep Time for the Pancakes: 15 minutes*
*Cooking Time to make all the Pancakes: 10 to 15 minutes*

2¼ cups flour

1½ teaspoons baking powder

½ teaspoon baking soda

½ teaspoon salt

1 tablespoon sugar, plus
1 teaspoon sugar

¼ stick (2 tablespoons)
butter, melted

2 large eggs

2½ cups buttermilk

semisweet chocolate chips

fresh strawberries, tossed
with sugar, to taste

confectioners sugar,
for garnish

1. In a large bowl, mix all the ingredients together, except the chocolate chips, fresh strawberries, and confectioners sugar.
2. In a separate bowl, toss the strawberries with sugar to bring out the juice. Set aside as a topping for the pancakes.
3. Preheat the griddle to 350°. Grease the griddle with butter. When water droplets dance briefly before disappearing, the griddle is ready for pancakes.
4. Ladle ⅓ to ½ cup of batter per pancake onto the griddle. Drop chocolate chips over each pancake.
5. Flip the pancakes when their tops are covered with bubbles that stay open. Check the underside to make sure it is nicely browned before flipping. Cook the other side for 2 to 3 minutes.
6. To serve, top the pancakes with strawberries, then sprinkle with confectioners sugar.

**Variation:** *Use frozen or fresh blueberries instead of chocolate chips.*

We had a saying at our Inn—"Most everything is better with buttermilk." Whether it was muffins, waffles, or pancakes that came out of our kitchen, you could be pretty sure there was buttermilk in it.

This is a great basic buttermilk pancake recipe that we often topped with a sauce or made with fresh blueberries instead of the chocolate chips. We started putting chocolate chips in the pancakes when one of our younger guests said he wanted chocolate for breakfast. Turns out most adults also like some chocolate for breakfast, especially when these pancakes are topped with fresh strawberries!

# Peach-Nectarine Upside-Down French Toast

ELLEN GUTMAN CHENAUX

*Serves 8*

*Prep Time: 15 minutes* ❧ *Chilling Time: 8 hours or overnight*
*Baking Time: 50 minutes* ❧ *Resting Time: 5 minutes*

1 stick (½ cup) unsalted butter

1 cup brown sugar, firmly packed

2 tablespoons light corn syrup

2 to 3 ripe but firm peaches, peeled and cut into ½-inch-thick slices

2 to 3 ripe but firm nectarines, peeled and cut into ½-inch-thick slices

1 loaf challah (egg bread)

4 eggs

1 cup whole milk

1 tablespoon vanilla extract

cinnamon/sugar

melon slices *or* berries, for garnish

1. Over medium-low heat, melt the butter in a large saucepan or skillet. Stir in the brown sugar and corn syrup, until the sugar has dissolved. Cook 3 to 5 minutes, until the mixture is thick and bubbly.
2. Remove the pan from the heat. Add the peaches and nectarines to the sauce, stirring gently until all the fruit is coated.
3. Spray a 9- x 13-inch glass baking pan with cooking spray. Add the fruit mixture, spreading it evenly over the bottom of the pan.
4. Slice the crust off the challah. Cut the challah into eight 1-inch-thick slices.
5. Place the slices in one layer over top of the fruit. Cover and refrigerate overnight.
6. When ready to bake, preheat the oven to 375°.
7. Whisk the eggs, milk, and vanilla together in a bowl. Pour over the bread slices. Sprinkle with cinnamon/sugar.
8. Bake for 50 minutes, until the top is golden brown and crisp.
9. Remove the French toast from the oven and let it stand 5 minutes before cutting.
10. Cut into 8 servings, inverting each serving onto an individual plate, fruit-side up. Spoon pan liquid over top. Serve with colorful melon slices or berries.

A terrific recipe for summer fruit!

# Cranberry French Toast

KATHRYN WHITE

*Serves 8*
*Prep Time: 25 minutes* ❧ *Chilling Time (optional): Overnight*
*Baking Time: 45 to 60 minutes*

## Cranberry Sauce Ingredients

12-ounce bag fresh cranberries

1 cup sugar

½ cup orange juice

1 teaspoon cinnamon

½ cup sweet orange marmalade

## French Toast Ingredients

1 stick (8 tablespoons) butter

1¼ cups brown sugar, lightly packed

¼ cup light corn syrup

1-pound loaf Italian bread, *or* other thickly sliced bread

8-ounce package cream cheese

8 eggs

1½ cups half-and-half

2 tablespoons orange juice

1 teaspoon vanilla

## Cranberry Sauce Instructions

1. Place the cranberries, sugar, orange juice, and cinnamon in a saucepan. Bring to a boil.
2. Reduce the heat and simmer until the cranberries start to pop.
3. Remove from the heat. Stir in the marmalade. Set aside.

## French Toast Instructions

1. Preheat the oven to 350° if baking immediately. Grease a 9- x 13- inch baking dish.
2. In a saucepan, melt the butter, brown sugar, and corn syrup together over low heat. Stir to blend.
3. Add 1 to 1½ cups of the homemade cranberry sauce to the brown sugar mixture. Set aside.
4. Slice the bread and spread cream cheese on one slice. Cover the spread side with another plain piece of bread, making a sandwich. Repeat until all the bread and cream cheese are used.
5. In a good-sized bowl, beat the eggs. Add the half-and-half, orange juice, and vanilla and blend together.

6. Spread a thin layer of the reserved cranberry/brown sugar mixture into the baking dish.
7. Layer the cream cheese sandwiches on top.
8. Pour the egg mixture over the sandwiches.
9. Refrigerate overnight, or bake immediately for a total of 45 to 60 minutes. First, bake covered with aluminum foil for 30 minutes; then remove foil and bake 15 to 30 minutes more, or until the bread is nicely browned.
10. Serve the French toast with a side of the remaining cranberry sauce, maple syrup, and your favorite bacon or sausage, if you wish.

This recipe idea came from a guest my first or second year as an innkeeper. After developing my own version, this French toast became a hit throughout the winter months when fresh cranberries are available.

# Decadent Chocolate French Toast with Strawberry Syrup

ELLEN GUTMAN CHENAUX

*Serves 4 (3 triangles per person)*
*Prep Time for the Syrup: 5 minutes   Prep Time for the French Toast: 20 minutes*
*Griddle Time: 5 to 7 minutes for each griddle-full*

### Strawberry Syrup Ingredients

¼ cup sugar

zest and juice of 1 lemon

1 cup fresh strawberries, or frozen, thawed

2 tablespoons Grand Marnier

### Strawberry Syrup Instructions

1. Add the syrup ingredients to a blender and purée.
2. Set aside.

## French Toast Ingredients

3 eggs

½ cup vanilla sugar, *or* ½ cup sugar, plus 1 teaspoon vanilla

2 tablespoons unsweetened cocoa powder

½ cup milk

¼ stick (2 tablespoons) butter

6 slices challah, each 1-inch thick, each cut on the diagonal for a total 12 triangles

### Garnish

unsweetened cocoa powder

whipped cream

4 strawberries, dipped in chocolate

confectioners sugar

## French Toast Instructions

1. Whisk the eggs together in a large bowl.
2. In a small bowl, combine the vanilla sugar (or sugar and vanilla) and cocoa powder until well blended.
3. Whisk the sugar/cocoa mixture into the eggs. Whisk in the milk.
4. Using a frying pan or griddle, melt the butter over medium heat.
5. Dip the triangles into the egg mixture, one at a time, until they're well moistened but not soggy. Place the triangles in pan or on the griddle, but don't crowd them.
6. Cook until they're golden, about 2 to 3 minutes per side, turning once. (This batter browns very quickly, so watch that the triangles don't burn.)

### To Serve:

1. Dust 4 individual dinner plates with cocoa powder.
2. Place one triangle flat on the plate. Place the second triangle on the plate, overlapping the first triangle. Repeat with the third triangle.
3. Drizzle with strawberry syrup. Add a dollop of whipped cream to the French toast.
4. Top with a chocolate-dipped strawberry.
5. Sprinkle with confectioners sugar and serve.

Chocolate for breakfast? You bet! Because you are using cocoa powder instead of chocolate, the French toast isn't sweet. But definitely use the strawberry sauce and fresh strawberries to make breakfast a special occasion.

This is a perfect breakfast for Valentine's Day!

# Outrageously Great Waffles— with Flavor Options

ELLEN GUTMAN CHENAUX

*Makes about 6 to 8 standard-sized waffles*
*Prep Time: 10 minutes ❧ Cooking Time: 4 to 5 minutes for each waffle*

¾ cup flour

¼ cup cornstarch

½ teaspoon baking powder

¼ teaspoon baking soda

¼ teaspoon salt

¾ teaspoon ground cinnamon

½ teaspoon ground ginger

¼ teaspoon freshly grated nutmeg

1 cup buttermilk

⅓ cup canola oil

1 extra-large egg

1½ teaspoons sugar

¾ teaspoon vanilla extract

1. In a medium-sized bowl, combine the flour, cornstarch, baking powder, baking soda, salt, cinnamon, ginger, and nutmeg. Mix well.
2. Add the buttermilk, oil, egg, sugar, and vanilla. Mix well.
3. Let the batter sit for about 30 minutes.
4. Spray the waffle iron very lightly with non-stick cooking spray. Pre-heat the waffle iron.
5. Following the waffle iron directions, cook the waffles.
6. Serve immediately with real maple syrup or with Bourbon Pecan Syrup (see recipe on page 214), or add rum to real maple syrup for a tropical flavor.

**Note:** *You can keep the waffles warm and crispy in a warm, or 300°, oven while you're making additional waffles.*

**Suggested Variations:**

1. *Lemon Waffles*: add the zest of one lemon to the batter in Step 2.
2. *Orange Waffles*: add the zest of one orange to the batter in Step 2.
3. *Berry Good Waffles*: Make a fruit sauce topping by adding some sugar to fresh or frozen blueberries, raspberries, strawberries, peaches...
4. *Caribbean Waffles*: Sauté sliced bananas or pineapple in butter. Spoon over the finished waffles and sprinkle with coconut. Or mix rum with real maple syrup as suggested above.
5. *Apple and Cinnamon Waffles*: Sauté sliced apples in butter. Add cinnamon. Use as a topping for the waffles.

The combinations are limitless!

For those who grew up on Eggos, you are in for a most special treat with these waffles! Flavorful, crunchy on the outside, and soft on the inside.

# Raised Waffles

DANIELLE HANSCOM

*Makes about 8 waffles*  ❧  *Prep Time: 15 minutes*
*Rising Time: 8 hours, or overnight*
*Standing Time: 15 minutes*  ❧  *Baking Time: 5 to 7 minutes*

¼ cup whole milk

1 tablespoon dry yeast

2 cups flour

2 tablespoons ground cornmeal

1 teaspoon salt

1 tablespoon granulated sugar

2 cups whole milk, lukewarm, at less than 110°

1 stick (8 tablespoons) unsalted butter, melted, and at room temperature

2 large eggs, lightly beaten

warm maple syrup

berries of your choice

1. Pour ¼ cup milk into a small bowl. Sprinkle the yeast on top. Let stand for 5 minutes. The yeast will dissolve and start to bubble.

2. In a separate large bowl, mix together the flour, cornmeal, salt, and sugar. Set aside.

3. Pour 2 cups of warmed milk (make sure the milk is less than 110° or it will kill the yeast) into another large bowl. Add the melted butter at room temperature, the eggs, and bubbly yeast mixture. Whisk until everything is well incorporated.

4. Add the flour mixture ½ cup at a time, whisking vigorously after each addition. The batter should be smooth.

5. Cover the bowl with plastic wrap. Set it on a large rimmed cookie tray to catch the overflow if necessary, because the batter will double in volume. Refrigerate overnight.

6. In the morning, preheat the waffle iron to high.

7. Whisk the batter; it will deflate. Let the batter rest for 15 minutes at room temperature.

8. Pour about ¾ cup of batter per waffle onto the hot waffle iron. Bake until the waffles are golden and their edges are crisp, about 5 to 7 minutes.

9. Serve topped with warm maple syrup or berries of your choice.

**Notes:**

*This batter will keep refrigerated for up to 3 days. Whisk it vigorously before each use.*

*These waffles are best made with a Belgian-type waffle maker.*

I have been serving these waffles for decades. They're a classic dish that never fails to delight. Top them with seasonal fruit and serve them for breakfast or dinner. Kids especially love them.

# Blueberry Pecan Waffles

DEBBIE MOSIMANN

*Makes three 8" Belgian-style waffles*
*Serves 6 (half of these large waffles is a serving)* ❧ *Prep Time: 10 minutes*
*Baking Time: 7 minutes, or until your waffle light turns off*

¾ cup flour

¼ cup coarsely ground pecans

¼ cup cornstarch

2 tablespoons sugar

½ teaspoon baking powder

¼ teaspoon baking soda

½ teaspoon salt

¼ teaspoon ground cinnamon

½ cup fresh blueberries,
small if possible

1 cup buttermilk

⅓ cup vegetable oil,
*or* melted butter

1 egg

½ teaspoon vanilla

**Note:** *Do not be tempted to substitute regular milk for the buttermilk!*

1. Preheat your waffle iron to High (if it has settings).
2. In a medium-sized bowl combine the flour, ground pecans, cornstarch, sugar, baking powder, baking soda, salt, and cinnamon. Using a wire whisk mix the ingredients together.
3. Toss the blueberries in the dry ingredients to coat them.
4. In a separate bowl mix the buttermilk, egg, oil, and vanilla together.
5. Add the wet ingredients to the dry ingredients. Stir gently, making sure all the flour is incorporated.
6. Spray the waffle iron with non-stick cooking spray or brush lightly with oil. This prevents the blueberries from sticking
7. Pour the batter onto the preheated waffle iron. The amount will depend on your waffle iron, but do not overfill it.
8. Bake until the light indicates that the waffle is done.
9. Carefully remove the waffle from the iron, split it in half, and serve immediately. Or hold on the warm setting of your grill or in a slightly warm (250°) oven until you're ready to serve.

These waffles are packed full of flavor with a perfect texture—soft on the inside and delightfully crisp on the outside. They are best served warm with a dollop of whipped cream and your favorite syrup.

When we make these for a group, we find they hold best on a griddle heated to warm or on the rack of a slightly warm oven.

Fresh blueberries work best; frozen ones tend to stick.

# Baked Oatmeal

DEBBIE MOSIMANN

*Serves 4*

*Prep Time: 10 minutes*  ✸  *Baking Time: 30 minutes*

½ cup oil (canola *or* corn, but not olive oil)

1 cup sugar

2 eggs

1½ cups quick-cooking oats (not instant)

1½ cups rolled oats

2 teaspoons baking powder

1 teaspoon salt

1 cup milk

1 teaspoon vanilla

1 teaspoon cinnamon

1½ cups mixed berries (blackberries, strawberries, blueberries)

milk for serving

1. Preheat your oven to 350°. Grease an 8- x 8-inch square baking pan.
2. Cream the oil, sugar, and eggs together in a medium-sized bowl.
3. Stir in the quick-cooking and rolled oats, the baking powder, salt, milk, vanilla, and cinnamon. Mix until well combined.
4. Pour half the batter into the greased baking dish.
5. Spoon the mixed berries evenly across the batter.
6. Top with remaining batter.
7. Bake uncovered for 30 minutes.
8. Serve warm with milk.

Baked Oatmeal is another Pennsylvania Dutch favorite. The recipe is simple and versatile. Top the batter with nuts, use any variety of fruit as a filling, or bake it plain without any toppings or fruit filling.
Our favorite filling is leftover Lemon Brandied Apples (see recipe on page 11).

# Griess Schnitten (Cream of Wheat Squares)

DEBBIE MOSIMANN

*Serves 8*
*Prep Time: 15 minutes ❧ Chilling Time: 2 hours, or overnight*
*Griddle Time: 10 to 12 minutes, per griddle-full*

4¼ cups milk

1 tablespoon butter

1 cup cream of wheat

½ teaspoon salt

1 teaspoon vanilla

1 tablespoon butter, for the griddle

1. Scald the milk, being careful not to let it boil. Add the butter to the milk.
2. While constantly whisking, add the cream of wheat to the hot milk in a slow stream. Stir in the salt.
3. Remove from the heat and stir in the vanilla.
4. Grease a 9- x 13-inch baking pan.
5. Pour the cream of wheat mixture into the pan while it's still hot.
6. Cover and chill for 2 hours, or until cold and set. At this point, it can be refrigerated overnight to use the next day.
7. Remove from the refrigerator and cut into 3-inch squares. Heat a skillet or griddle until a drop of water bounces.
8. Add 1 tablespoon of butter to the griddle. As soon as it has melted, but before it browns, arrange the squares on the griddle.
9. Fry the squares for 5 to 10 minutes, or until golden brown on the bottom, being careful not to check too soon.
10. Flip and fry on the other side until golden brown.
11. Serve hot with applesauce or a fruit compote and cinnamon/sugar.

*In Switzerland we used leftover cream of wheat to make these fabulous squares for a light supper. They are most often served hot with applesauce or a fruit compote and a generous sprinkling of cinnamon sugar.*

# Orange Blintz Bake

YVONNE MARTIN

*Serves 8 to 12*
*Prep Time: 30 minutes* ✆ *Baking Time: 40 minutes*

## Cream Cheese Filling Ingredients

8-ounce package cream cheese,
at room temperature

1 cup small curd cottage
cheese *or* ricotta

1 egg

1 tablespoon sugar

1 teaspoon vanilla

2 tablespoons frozen orange
juice concentrate, *optional*

½ cup orange marmalade (microwaved
for a few seconds to soften it)

1½ cups blueberries, fresh *or* frozen

## Blintz Batter Ingredients

1 stick (½ cup) butter, at
room temperature

⅓ cup sugar

1. Preheat oven to 350°. Grease a 9- x 13-inch baking pan.
2. In one bowl, make the filling by beating together the cream cheese, cottage cheese, 1 egg, 1 tablespoon sugar, vanilla, and orange juice concentrate if you wish. Set mixture aside.
3. In a second good-sized bowl, make the batter by creaming the butter and ⅓ cup sugar together.
4. Add 4 eggs one at a time, beating well after each addition.
5. Add flour, baking powder, yogurt, and sour cream, mixing well and scraping the bowl down.
6. Pour half of the batter into the prepared pan.
7. Pour all of the cream cheese filling over the batter.
8. Dot with dollops of orange marmalade. Sprinkle blueberries over top.
9. Cover with the remainder of the batter.

4 eggs

1 cup sifted flour

2 teaspoons baking powder

1 cup plain *or* vanilla yogurt

½ cup sour cream

10. Bake for about 40 minutes, or until the Blintz is set in the center and golden brown on top.
11. Let cool at least 10 minutes before cutting and serving.

*While there are quite a few steps to this recipe, it's well worth the effort. And it's great for brunch.*

# Caramel Peach Bread Pudding

YVONNE MARTIN

*Serves 12*

*Prep Time: 30 minutes* ✂ *Baking Time: 40 to 50 minutes*

**For the Bread Pudding:**

4 cups sliced peaches, frozen, fresh, *or* canned

12 large eggs

1 cup evaporated milk

½ cup 2% milk

1 teaspoon vanilla

1 teaspoon almond extract

2 tablespoons sugar

about 10 slices Italian *or* French bread, cut into ¾-inch cubes (you may need more *or* less, depending on the size of the loaf of bread)

**For the Topping:**

half a stick (¼ cup) butter

2 tablespoons corn syrup

1 cup brown sugar, lightly packed

¾ cup chopped pecans

1. Preheat your oven to 350°. Spray a 9- x 13-inch baking pan with non-stick cooking spray.
2. Place the peaches in a single layer on the bottom of the baking pan.
3. In a large bowl, mix the eggs, evaporated milk, 2% milk, vanilla, almond extract, and sugar together. Beat well.
4. Stir the bread cubes into the egg batter. Use just enough cubes so that they are saturated, with some liquid left in the bowl. Spoon the bread mixture over the peaches.
5. Meanwhile, melt the butter for the topping in a medium saucepan. Mix in the corn syrup and brown sugar. Bring to a simmer over medium heat, stirring constantly.
6. Remove from the heat and stir in the pecans. Drizzle the topping evenly over the bread mixture.
7. Cover with foil. Bake for 40 minutes.
8. Remove the foil and continue baking until the center is set. Test by sticking a knife blade into the center of the pudding. If no egg batter runs out, the pudding is done.
9. Serve warm.

We often have partial loaves of bread left over after dinner service at the inn.
We cut them into cubes and store them in the freezer to use in this recipe.

# Blueberry Bread Pudding with Orange Custard

DEBBIE MOSIMANN

*Serves 8*

*Prep Time for bread pudding: 15 minutes  ✷  Soaking Time: 8 hours, or overnight*
*Prep Time for custard: 10 minutes  ✷  Cooling Time: 15 to 20 minutes*

1½ cups blueberries

2 tablespoons orange liqueur (Triple Sec *or* Grand Marnier)

8 slices white bread, cubed, *divided*

8-ounce package cream cheese, cubed, *divided*

1½ cups milk

8 eggs

¼ cup honey

1 teaspoon orange zest

half a stick (¼ cup) butter, melted, *optional* (but really, really good!)

fresh berries, lightly sweetened

orange liqueur

1. Place berries in a bowl. Add the orange liqueur and toss gently together.
2. Butter a 9- x 9-inch baking dish. Place half the cubed bread in the bottom of the baking dish.
3. Layer with half the marinated berries and half the cubed cream cheese.
4. Cover with half the remaining bread cubes, and all of the remaining berries and cream cheese cubes. Top with the rest of the bread cubes.
5. Mix the milk, eggs, honey, and orange zest in a bowl. Pour over the bread layers, berries, and cheese.
6. Cover and refrigerate for 8 hours, or overnight.
7. Remove from the refrigerator half an hour before baking. Drizzle with melted butter if you wish.
8. Preheat your oven to 350°. Cover the baking dish with foil and bake 30 minutes.
9. Uncover and bake an additional 15 to 20 minutes, or until a toothpick comes out clean when inserted into the center of the pudding.
10. Allow the pudding to cool to warm or room temperature before serving.
11. Cut into squares. Serve with the Orange Custard (recipe follows) and lightly sweetened fresh berries, drizzled with a bit of orange liqueur.

# Orange Custard

*Makes 2 cups*

2 cups milk

1 egg

1 egg yolk

¼ cup sugar

1 tablespoon cornstarch

1 teaspoon orange zest

1 teaspoon vanilla extract

pinch of salt

1. Scald 2 cups of milk in a small saucepan.
2. In a small bowl, beat the egg, egg yolk, sugar, and cornstarch together until smooth and without lumps.
3. When the milk is hot, add half of it to the egg mixture, stirring until smooth.
4. Slowly pour the egg/milk mixture into the remaining hot milk in the saucepan and return it to the burner.
5. Cook over medium heat, stirring constantly, until it starts to thicken. The custard is finished when it thickens and coats a spoon but has not boiled.
6. Remove from heat. Stir in the orange zest, vanilla, and a pinch of salt.
7. Stir at intervals until the custard has cooled, but is still warm.
8. Serve with the warm bread pudding. Refrigerate any remaining custard.

**Notes:** *Fresh or frozen blueberries work well.*

*If you're feeling creative, mix in some fresh peaches or blackberries to give it a tart note.*

*If we have left-over croissants, we often sprinkle them, diced, on top to add a beautiful crust.*

When we serve this for breakfast, we call it Baked Blueberry French Toast, but because the bread is soaked overnight, it's really a bread pudding.

# Scandinavian Apple Pancake

## LYNNETTE SCOFIELD

*Serves 4 to 6*

*Prep Time: 20 minutes*  ✾  *Cooking Time: 10 minutes*  ✾  *Baking Time: 25 to 35 minutes*

¾ stick (6 tablespoons) butter

2 large apples, your choice of variety

¼ cup sugar

1 teaspoon lemon zest

pinch of cinnamon

½ cup water

½ cup whipping cream

3 large eggs

1¼ cups flour

¾ teaspoon baking powder

½ cup confectioners sugar

1 teaspoon salt

1. Preheat the oven to 250°.
2. Melt the butter over medium-high heat in a non-stick 8- or 9-inch skillet that is oven-safe.
3. Peel and slice the apples into the melted butter. Sauté for 5 minutes.
4. Stir in the sugar, lemon zest, and cinnamon. Sauté for another 5 minutes.
5. In a bowl, whisk the water, cream, and eggs together till well blended.
6. In a separate bowl, whisk the flour, baking powder, confectioners sugar, and salt together.
7. Pour the egg mixture into the dry ingredients. Whisk into a batter.
8. Make sure the apples are distributed evenly over the bottom of the pan.
9. Remove the pan from the stove and gently pour the batter over the apples, being careful not to displace them.
10. Bake at 250° for 10 minutes. Then increase the oven temperature to 425°. Continue to bake for another 15 to 20 minutes. The pancake is finished when a toothpick inserted into the center comes out clean. It will be golden brown.
11. Have a serving plate ready. Remove the skillet from the oven. Place the plate over the skillet and carefully and quickly invert the pancake onto the plate. Serve immediately.

When apples are in season, this pancake is especially a hit. The lemon gives it a bright flavor. I love it with just a bit of cinnamon, but if you're a cinnamon lover, go ahead and add more (up to 1 tsp).

# Savory Breakfasts

## Get Crackin'

# Omelet with Variations

KATHRYN WHITE

*Serves 1*

**For the Basic Omelet:**

2 to 3 eggs

1 tablespoon water

1 tablespoon butter

salt and pepper, to taste

**Note:** *Chopped parsley, thyme, scallions, garlic, and rosemary are flavorful additions.*

1. Break eggs into a small bowl. Break the yolks with a whisk or fork.
2. Add water and whisk until just blended.
3. Heat a nonstick 8-inch skillet with sloped sides over medium heat, then add the butter and melt. The butter should sizzle slightly.
4. Pour the eggs into the skillet. In 15 seconds, using a heat-proof spatula, pull the set eggs to the center of the skillet. This allows the unset eggs to cook. Watch carefully and lower the heat, if necessary, to prevent the eggs from burning.
5. Add herbs, cheese, or fillings when the top thin layer of eggs is still moist. Using the spatula, fold the omelet in half, or fold one-third over the middle, and then the other third over the middle.
6. Slide the omelet out of the pan by tilting it over the plate.

**For a spinach and mushroom omelet:**

1. Sauté ¼ cup sliced mushrooms in a lightly coated nonstick skillet.
2. After 2 minutes, add ½ cup chopped fresh spinach and cook until the spinach wilts. Remove from the skillet and set aside.
3. Follow directions for the basic omelet.
4. Add the spinach and mushroom filling. Add ¼ cup grated Gruyère cheese. Fold and serve.

**For a bacon, apple, and cheddar omelet:**

1. Cook 2 slices of bacon until crisp. Drain on a paper towel. Wipe out the bacon drippings and add ½ tablespoon of butter.
2. Sauté half an apple that has been peeled, cored, and thinly sliced. After cooking for about 3 minutes, until tender, place apples in a small dish and set aside.
3. Follow directions for the basic omelet.
4. Add bacon and apple as a filling, and spread with 2 tablespoons of grated sharp cheddar cheese. Fold and serve.

**Other combinations:**

1. Asparagus and crumbled goat cheese; zucchini and tomato; and broccoli and caramelized onions; in combination with crumbled feta or Parmigiano-Reggiano, Swiss, or cheddar cheese.
2. Roasted red peppers, squash, and other veggies can be used.

# Caramelized Onion Omelet

DANIELLE HANSCOM

*Serves 4*
*Prep Time: 20 minutes* ✿ *Cooking Time: 1 to 1¼ hours*

2 large sweet onions, such as Vidalias

2 tablespoons good olive oil

1 tablespoon unsalted butter

3-inch twig fresh rosemary

8 large eggs

sea salt and a few grindings of black pepper, to taste

2 tablespoons heavy cream, *divided*

4 teaspoons unsalted butter, *divided*

1 cup coarsely grated smoked Gouda

1. Dice onions into ¼-inch pieces to make approximately 5 cups.
2. Melt olive oil and 1 tablespoon butter in a large frying pan over medium-high heat until butter and olive oil start to foam.
3. Add diced onion. Reduce heat and cook slowly for 45 to 60 minutes, stirring every 5 minutes or so to make sure the onions don't burn. They should have a dark golden color when done. Remove from heat and set aside.

   (Onions have a high sugar content, which gives them their incredible flavor when cooked slowly. But it can also cause them to burn if they're cooked too fast.)
4. Remove rosemary leaves from stem and chop very finely. Add to caramelized onions and mix well.
5. In a 2-cup measuring cup, vigorously whisk together 2 eggs, salt and pepper to taste, ½ tablespoon heavy cream.
6. Melt 1teaspoon butter in an 8-inch nonstick omelet pan over medium- high heat. When butter stops foaming, add whisked eggs and let set for 30 seconds. Then, using a heatproof spatula, lift eggs from the side to the center to ensure that they are cooking evenly and not cooking dry around the edges.
7. Distribute one-quarter of caramelized onions/rosemary mixture over half the omelet. Sprinkle with ¼ cup grated cheese.
8. Fold omelet in half and keep warm. Repeat the same procedure for the other 3 omelets.
9. Serve immediately.

Caramelizing onions takes time, but is well worth the effort,
and it is a task you can do a day ahead.

**Note:** *This is just one suggested filling. We often use cheddar and apples, sautéing the apples before adding them to the omelet. Or use your favorite omelet fillings. Be creative!*

*Not only does this recipe taste delicious but the presentation gets bravos! And you can add any filling you like. Truly an omelet for all seasons.*

# Ham and Cheese Rolled Omelet

ELLEN GUTMAN CHENAUX

*Serves 6*

*Prep Time: 10 minutes* ✦ *Baking Time: 15 to 20 minutes*

4 ounces (half an 8-ounce package) cream cheese, softened and cut into chunks

¾ cup whole milk

2 tablespoons flour

¼ teaspoon kosher salt

12 large eggs

**Filling Ingredients**

2 tablespoons Dijon mustard

2 cups grated cheddar cheese, *divided*

1½ cups diced cooked ham

½ cup sliced green onions

1. Preheat oven to 375°.
2. Grease the bottom of a jelly roll pan (15 x 10 x 1-inch) with nonstick cooking spray. Line the bottom of the jelly roll pan with parchment paper, making sure to have the paper going up the sides. Grease the parchment paper with nonstick cooking spray, too.
3. In a blender, blend the cream cheese and milk until smooth. Add the flour and salt and blend to combine.
4. Beat the eggs in a bowl until well mixed. Add the eggs to the cream cheese mixture in the blender. Blend well.
5. Place the prepared jelly roll pan on the middle rack of the oven to preheat (for about 5 minutes).
6. Remove heated pan from the oven. Carefully pour the egg mixture into the pan. Bake for 15 to 20 minutes, or until the eggs are set and puffed.
7. Remove the pan from the oven and immediately spread the top of the eggs with mustard. Sprinkle with 1¾ cups of cheese. Then sprinkle with the ham and green onions.
8. Roll up the omelet from the short side, peeling the parchment paper away while rolling.
9. Sprinkle the top with the remaining ¼ cup cheese. Return the omelet to the oven for 3 to 4 minutes to melt the cheese.
10. Slice the omelet into 6 slices and serve.

# Tri-Color Terrine

ELLEN GUTMAN CHENAUX AND DEBBIE MOSIMANN

*Serves 6-8*
*Prep. Time: 1 hour  ✻  Bake Time: 1 hour*

3 medium red bell peppers, roasted or baked, peeled, and cut into small pieces

3 tablespoons extra-virgin olive oil, *divided*

1 tablespoon finely chopped fresh basil

salt and pepper, to taste

2 pounds green Swiss chard, *or* kale

¼ cup finely chopped shallot

salt and pepper, to taste

13 large eggs, *divided*

⅔ teaspoon kosher salt, *divided*

¾ cup crème fraîche, *or* heavy cream, *divided*

1½ cups grated aged cheddar

1. Sauté the peppers in 1½ tablespoons of hot oil. Stir often until the peppers are tender and the liquid has evaporated.
2. Add the basil, salt, and pepper to taste. Transfer the vegetables to a bowl and let them cool.
3. Cook the chard or kale in a large pot of boiling, salted water until tender, about 2 to 3 minutes.
4. Drain; then rinse under cold water. Squeeze the chard or kale to remove as much moisture as possible. Chop.
5. In a large skillet, cook the shallot in 1½ tablespoons of oil, stirring until the shallot softens and begins to brown.
6. Add the chard or kale, stirring until the mixture looks dry, about 2 to 3 minutes. Add salt and pepper to taste. Cool, then cover and chill.
   **Note:** The above can be prepared the day before serving the terrine.
7. When you're ready to prepare the whole terrine, preheat the oven to 450°.
8. Remove the bowls of vegetables from the refrigerator and let them warm to room temperature.
9. Crack 4 eggs into 1 bowl and 4 eggs into a second bowl.
10. Add ⅓ teaspoon of salt, plus pepper to taste, to each bowl, and then whisk.

11. Whisk 3 tablespoons of crème fraîche/heavy cream into a one bowl of eggs and whisk until smooth. Add the red peppers and stir.

12. Whisk 3 tablespoons of creme fraiche/heavy cream into the second bowl of eggs until smooth. Add the chard or kale mixture and stir.

13. Pour the red pepper-egg mixture into an oiled 12- x 4-inch loaf pan. Place the loaf pan in a hot water bath (2 inches of water in a roasting pan large enough to hold the loaf pan) for 20 minutes, or until firm.

14. Pour the chard or kale mixture into the loaf pan and bake (again in a hot water bath) for 20 minutes, or until firm.

15. Crack the remaining eggs into a bowl. Whisk in salt and pepper to taste.

16. Stir in the grated cheddar cheese and the remaining crème fraîche or cream. Pour this mixture into the loaf pan. Bake in a hot water bath until the eggs are lightly brown and slightly puffed, about 20 minutes.

17. Remove the loaf pan from the oven. Cool on a rack for 3 minutes.

18. Invert the omelet onto a cutting board. Cut it into 8 slices, and serve.

*Notes:*

*If you plan to make this omelet on the morning you're going to serve it, you can make the red pepper and chard/kale layers a day ahead, covering and chilling them in separate bowls.*

*You can also bake the whole terrine the day before you're going to serve it. In fact, this makes it easier to slice. Just reheat the slices.*

There are oohs and aahs every time we serve this omelet. Although this is a time-consuming recipe, it is not difficult and it's definitely worth the time. It is a healthy special occasion breakfast or brunch entrée.

**Note:** *Use any combination of vegetables and cheese.*
*Any veggies in season work perfectly for this dish!*

I love making and serving frittatas—the options are endless, and with great spices, this dish bursts with flavor. A veggie frittata works well for diverse groups of people with food restrictions. Gluten-free and vegetarian guests are extremely happy with this tasty dish. The frittata, moreover, is not only for breakfast or brunch; it is a great supper treat, too.

# Veggie Frittata

KRISTIE ROSSET

*Serves 6 to 8*
*Prep Time: 30 minutes* ✋ *Cooking Time: 10 to 15 minutes*

12 large eggs

2 tablespoons half-and-half

3 tablespoons melted butter

½ teaspoon salt

⅛ teaspoon pepper

⅓ cup grated Parmesan cheese

3 tablespoons olive oil

⅓ cup quartered artichoke hearts

⅓ cup diced green onions

⅓ cup diced red bell pepper

⅓ cup diced asparagus

1½ cups chopped fresh spinach

¾ cup grated Monterey
Jack cheese and/or
cheddar cheese, *divided*

1 teaspoon chopped fresh parsley

*Serve it with salsa if you wish.*

1. Preheat oven to broil. Position the oven rack so the skillet filled with the frittata will be approximately 5 inches below the broiler.
2. In a good-sized bowl, whisk together the eggs, half-and-half, melted butter, salt, pepper, and Parmesan cheese.
3. Coat the bottom of a 10-inch, oven-safe skillet generously with olive oil. With the heat on high, sauté the artichoke hearts, green onions, bell pepper, and asparagus until tender. Stir in the chopped fresh spinach.
4. Pour the eggs over the vegetables. Add half of the grated cheese.
5. Lift edges of the eggs to allow liquid eggs to run underneath. Continue to lift the edges until all the eggs are firm, but still wet on top.
6. Sprinkle the remaining grated cheese on top, and then sprinkle with parsley.
7. Place the pan under broiler for 4 to 5 minutes, until the frittata is lightly golden brown.
8. Slide the frittata out of the pan and onto a cutting surface. Allow it to rest for 1 minute. Then cut and serve.

# Summer Frittata

YVONNE MARTIN

*Serves 6 (1 pie)*
*Prep Time: 30 minutes* ❧ *Baking Time: 40 minutes* ❧ *Standing Time: 10 minutes*

¼ stick (2 tablespoons) butter

1 cup diced onion

1 large yellow *or* green zucchini, sliced into ¼-inch-thick slices

1 teaspoon dried basil

1 teaspoon dried oregano

5 eggs

¾ cup milk

¼ cup flour

1 teaspoon baking powder

1 cup fresh diced tomatoes

½ cup shredded cheddar cheese

1 cup crumbled feta cheese

1. Preheat the oven to 350°.
2. Melt the butter in a skillet. Sauté the onion in it until translucent.
3. Add the zucchini. Sprinkle with basil and oregano. Sauté for about 3 or 4 minutes.
4. Combine the eggs, milk, flour, and baking powder in a blender or food processor.
5. Spray a 9-inch pie plate with cooking spray. Spread the onion/zucchini mixture in the bottom of the pie plate. Spread the diced tomatoes, cheddar, and feta cheeses evenly over top. Gently pour the egg batter over all.
6. Bake for about 40 minutes, or until set in the middle. Let stand for 10 minutes before slicing into 6 wedges.

**Note:** *If fresh herbs are in season, substitute 2 tablespoons shredded basil and 2 teaspoons fresh oregano leaves for the dried.*

This is one of our go-to recipes at the inn. We make many variations, changing the vegetables and cheeses based on what's in season, and in our refrigerator!

# Tomato Basil Pie

ELLEN GUTMAN CHENAUX

*Serves 6*
*Prep Time: 30 minutes*
*Baking Time: 20 minutes to pre-bake the pie crust, plus 60 minutes for the filled pie*
*Resting Time: 5 to 10 minutes*

3 to 4 large tomatoes

½ teaspoon kosher salt

¼ teaspoon freshly
ground black pepper

1 cup fresh basil

¾ cup ricotta cheese

4 large eggs, lightly beaten

2 cups grated
Parmesan cheese

additional salt and freshly
ground black pepper, to taste

9-inch unbaked pie shell

**The day before serving:**

1. Slice the tomatoes about ¼-inch thick. Place the slices and ends on a baking sheet lined with a double layer of paper towels. Sprinkle the tomatoes lightly with kosher salt and pepper. Cover with a double layer of paper towels. Cover with plastic wrap and refrigerate overnight.
2. In a food processor, purée the basil and ricotta together. Add the eggs and blend. Pour the mixture into a bowl.
3. Stir in the Parmesan cheese, additional salt, and pepper to taste, and combine.
4. Refrigerate mixture covered overnight.

**Note:** *This recipe is also great as individual tarts.*

*Tomatoes and fresh basil shout "Summer!"
And this is a great way to enjoy these
summer favorites.*

**The day of serving the pie:**

1. Preheat the oven to 400°.
2. Prick the sides and bottom of the pie shell with a fork. Spray a sheet of foil with cooking spray and place sprayed side down on the pie shell. Fill the pie shell with baking beans. Prebake the pie shell for 20 minutes.
3. Remove the pie shell from the oven. Remove the beans and foil. Line the bottom of the pie crust with the end slices of tomato.
4. Pour the ricotta mixture over the tomatoes.
5. Arrange the remaining tomato slices on top of the ricotta mixture in one overlapping layer.
6. Sprinkle a bit more Parmesan cheese on the tomatoes.
7. Spray the pie lightly with nonstick cooking spray. If needed, protect the edges of the pie with a pie crust saver or aluminum foil. Bake for 1 hour at 400°, or until set and lightly browned.
8. Remove from the oven. Let sit for 5 to 10 minutes before slicing into 6 servings.
9. Serve hot or at room temperature.

# Have you tried these?

Upside-Down Sour Cherry Muffins, page 48

Parmesan Heirloom Cherry Tomatoes, page 198

Honey Oat Bread, page 74

French Hot Chocolate, page 234

# Asparagus Goat Cheese Crustless Quiche

KATHRYN WHITE

*Serves 6*
*Prep Time: 10 to 12 minutes   Baking Time: 45 minutes*

12 ounces fresh
asparagus, trimmed

2 tablespoons olive oil

½ teaspoon Herbes
de Provence

4 ounces goat
cheese, crumbled

5 large eggs

1¼ cups half-and-half

pinch of salt
(I use kosher)

¼ teaspoon freshly
ground pepper

1. Preheat oven to 375°. Spray a 9-inch pie plate with nonstick cooking spray, or grease with a favorite oil.
2. Prepare asparagus by cutting the stems into ½-inch pieces.
3. In medium skillet, heat olive oil over medium heat and add asparagus. Sauté for 2 minutes.
4. Place asparagus in bottom of pie plate. Sprinkle Herbes de Provence over asparagus. Crumble goat cheese over top.
5. In large bowl, whisk eggs until light. Stir in half-and-half. Season with salt and pepper to taste. Pour over asparagus and cheese.
6. Bake at 375° until quiche is puffed and lightly brown, 40 to 45 minutes, or until a knife inserted into center of quiche comes out clean.
7. Serve warm.

*There are numerous veggie and cheese combinations for quiche, but this is my all-time favorite.*

# Mediterranean Quiche

JOYCE SCHULTE

*Serves 12*
*Prep Time: 35 minutes*
*Baking Time: 30 minutes for ramekins; 40 to 45 minutes for pie pans*

10 eggs

½ cup flour

1 teaspoon baking powder

half a stick (4 tablespoons) butter, melted

3 cups cottage cheese

1 cup grated cheddar cheese

10-ounce box frozen chopped spinach, thawed and squeezed dry

1 cup chopped roasted red peppers

1 tablespoon dried oregano

Tabasco sauce, to taste

salt and black pepper, to taste

1 cup crumbled feta cheese

1. Preheat the oven to 375°.
2. Beat eggs in a large mixing bowl. Stir in flour, baking powder, and melted butter. Mix well. The batter will still be lumpy.
3. Stir in cottage cheese, cheddar cheese, spinach, roasted red peppers, oregano, and other seasonings, blending well.
4. Divide mixture into 12 greased, 6-ounce round ramekins, or divide the mixture into two 8-inch greased pie pans.
5. Sprinkle the tops with feta cheese.
6. Bake for 30 minutes at 375°. The tops should be lightly browned.

**Note:** *Try adding ⅓ cup of Kalamata olives to the egg mixture for those who love olives like I do.*

We've been big on crustless quiches at our inn: I was never very fond of making pie crusts, although my husband was quite good at it. And most of our guests just ate the inside and left the crust, wanting to skip the calories and carbs in the crust and focus on the good filling instead. So we started focusing on the egg dish itself and found baking it in individual ramekins, or in a pie pan without a crust, made us and our guests happy.

# Maryland Blue Crab Quiche

DANIELLE HANSCOM

*Serves 8 for breakfast; 6 for lunch*
*Prep Time: 30 minutes total ✌ Baking Time: 55 to 65 minutes total*
*Cooling Time: 35 minutes total*

**For the pastry:**

1¼ cups flour

1 stick (8 tablespoons)
cold unsalted butter,
cut into ½-inch cubes

¼ teaspoon salt

3 to 8 tablespoons
ice water

*For all the seafood
lovers. This quiche is
perfect for breakfast,
lunch, or dinner*

**To make the pastry:**

1. Preheat the oven to 375°.
2. In a food processor, pulse together the flour, butter, and salt until mixture resembles coarse meal.
3. Drizzle with 3 tablespoons of ice water. Pulse 3 to 4 times until incorporated.
4. Squeeze a small handful of pastry. If it doesn't hold together, add more ice water, ½ tablespoon at a time, pulsing until just incorporated. Test again. Do not overwork the mixture or the pastry will be tough.
5. Turn the mixture out onto a work surface and divide it into 4 portions. With the heel of your hand, smear each portion once or twice in a forward motion to help distribute the fat.
6. Gather the dough together with a scraper and press it into a ball. Then flatten the ball into a 4-inch disk. Wrap the dough with plastic wrap and chill, until firm, for about 1 hour.
7. Roll out the dough into a round, approximately 12 inches across, on a lightly floured surface.
8. Line a deep-dish glass pie plate with the pastry.
9. Fold the overhang of dough under the pastry and press against the rim of the pie plate to reinforce the edge. Crimp the edge.

**For the filling:**

8 large eggs

1 cup half-and-half

1 cup heavy cream

2 tablespoons finely chopped fresh chives

2 tablespoons finely chopped fresh parsley

1 tablespoon finely chopped fresh lovage

½ teaspoon Old Bay seasoning

½ teaspoon salt

¼ teaspoon freshly ground black pepper

⅛ teaspoon freshly grated nutmeg

1 pound lump crabmeat, picked over and cleared of any shell

4 ounces grated fontina, Monterey Jack, *or* any other mild cheese

10. Prick the bottom and side of the pastry with a fork. Freeze until firm, for about 20 minutes.
11. Line the pie shell with foil and fill with pie weights. Bake until the pastry is set underneath the foil, for about 15 minutes.
12. Remove the foil and weights. Continue baking the shell until its bottom and sides are lightly golden, for about 10 minutes more.
13. Remove from the oven and cool completely on a wire rack.

**To make the filling:**

1. Reduce the oven temperature to 350°.
2. In a good-sized bowl, whisk together the eggs, half-and-half, heavy cream, herbs, Old Bay seasoning, salt, pepper, and nutmeg.
3. Place the pie plate on a rimmed baking sheet. Layer the crust with crabmeat and cheese.
4. Pour the egg mixture over top and bake at 350° until the filling puffs, for 40 to 50 minutes. When finished, it should no longer be wobbly in the center.
5. Remove from the oven. Cool on a rack for at least 15 minutes before cutting and serving the quiche warm.

Since retiring from innkeeping,
whenever I hear the words,
"Northwest Salmon Breakfast Pie,"
I think, "That is one of the best
dishes we ever made!"

Poaching the fresh salmon brings
out its natural flavor and makes
this dish unique. Add to that the
Swiss cheese and the sour cream,
and you have amazing taste.

# Northwest Salmon Breakfast Pie

JOYCE SCHULTE

*Serves 6*
*Prep Time: 20 minutes* ❧ *Baking Time: 53 to 55 minutes*
*Standing Time: 15 minutes*

9" pie crust

12 ounces fully cooked salmon

1 cup chopped onions

1 garlic clove, minced

3 tablespoons butter

5 eggs

¼ cup flour

2¼ cups sour cream

1½ cups shredded Swiss cheese, *divided*

1 teaspoon dried dill

1. Preheat the oven to 400°.
2. Bake the pie crust for 8 minutes. Remove from the oven. Reduce the oven temperature to 375°.
3. Remove any skin and bones from the salmon; then flake it into small pieces.
4. In a medium skillet, over low-medium heat, sauté the onion and garlic in butter until tender.
5. Add the sautéed onion and garlic to the salmon and mix well but gently.
6. In a good-sized bowl, whisk the eggs and flour together. Add the sour cream and mix well.
7. Add the salmon and onion mixture and stir until blended. Add 1 cup of Swiss cheese and the dill. Blend gently.
8. Pour the mixture into the partially baked crust. Sprinkle with the remaining cheese.
9. Bake uncovered at 400° for 30 minutes, and then cover with foil. Bake for another 15 minutes or until the mixture is set.
10. Let stand for 15 minutes before slicing and serving it warm.

# Spinach and Leek Soufflé

DEBBIE MOSIMANN

*Serves 8*
*Prep Time: 15 minutes*
*Baking Time: 45 minutes for a large baking dish; 15 minutes for individual dishes*

8-ounce package cream cheese, softened to room temperature

1 cup sour cream

2 tablespoons flour

⅛ teaspoon pepper

2 cups shredded aged, sharp cheddar cheese

12 ounces cottage cheese

1 large leek, *or* an onion, *or* spring onions

3 cups roughly chopped fresh spinach with stems removed

**Note:** *Fresh spinach is a must here.*

1. In a good-sized bowl, mix together the cream cheese and sour cream until well blended.
2. Stir in the flour, pepper, and shredded cheddar cheese until well mixed.
3. Stir in the cottage cheese, but be careful not to over-mix. You want to keep the consistency of the cottage cheese.
4. At this point, you can cover and hold the mixture overnight in the refrigerator to bake in the morning.
5. When ready to bake, preheat the oven to 350°. Slice the leek, leaving the rings whole. Use up through the white part of the leek, just until it starts to turn a darker green. If using onions, dice them.
6. Fold the spinach and leeks into the egg and cheese mixture.
7. Pour it into a 2-quart baking dish that has been greased, sprayed, or buttered.
8. Bake at 350° for about 45 minutes. The finished casserole should be somewhat puffed, a toothpick inserted into its center should come out almost clean, and the edges will be brown.

   Or divide the mixture among 8 6-ounce ramekins. Bake for 15 minutes, or until finished as described above.
9. At this stage, the dish will hold in a warm oven until you're ready to serve it. Close the door and turn the oven off. Serve hot.

The leek rings give it a great appearance, but if you can't find them, use chopped onions.

This can be mixed up the day before serving, but do not add the spinach and leeks until right before baking.

# Fondue Florentine Soufflé

ELLEN GUTMAN CHENAUX

*Serves 8*

*Prep Time: 30 minutes* ❧ *Baking Time: 45 minutes*

10-ounce box frozen chopped spinach, thawed and squeezed to remove as much liquid as possible

¼ stick (2 tablespoons) unsalted butter

2 large shallots, minced, *or* 1 large onion chopped

freshly ground black pepper

5 cups French bread cubes (½- to ¾-inch in size), lightly toasted, *divided*

½ pound Gruyere cheese, coarsely grated, *divided*

15 large eggs

3½ cups whole milk

1 teaspoon Maggi Seasoning (found in most supermarkets; used by Europeans for flavor, often instead of salt), *or* 1 teaspoon salt

2 tablespoons Dijon mustard

pepper to taste

**The day before serving:**

1. Grease 8 8-ounce ramekins with cooking spray.
2. Melt the butter in a skillet over medium heat and sauté the shallots or onions until somewhat translucent.
3. Add the spinach. Add pepper to taste.
4. Place 3 or 4 bread cubes at the bottom of each ramekin.
5. Add one heaping tablespoon of the onion-spinach mixture on top of the bread.
6. Sprinkle half of the cheese on top of the onion-spinach mixture.
7. Add 3 or 4 more bread cubes on top of the cheese in each ramekin.
8. Divide the onion-spinach mixture among the 8 ramekins, and then the remaining cheese.
9. Crack the eggs in a large bowl. Add the milk, Maggi seasoning, Dijon mustard, and pepper to taste. Whisk well.
10. Divide the egg mixture evenly among the 8 ramekins, filling each one just about to the top.
11. Cover the ramekins with plastic wrap and refrigerate overnight, or freeze for up to 2 weeks.

**The day of serving:**

1.  An hour before serving, preheat the oven to 375°. Remove the soufflés from the refrigerator.
2.  Place the ramekins in the oven <u>directly</u> on the rack (not on a baking sheet) and bake for 45 minutes, or until lightly browned.
3.  Serve immediately before the soufflé deflates.

*At one time, this was Birchwood Inn's signature dish, adapted from my father-in-law's fondue recipe. This dish always rises to the occasion.*

# Garden Baked Eggs

JOYCE SCHULTE

*Serves 6*
*Prep Time: 25 minutes* ✋ *Baking Time: 20 to 30 minutes*

12 eggs

½ cup half-and-half

salt and pepper, to taste

thyme (dried *or* fresh), to taste

2 cups fresh, seasonal vegetables, chopped, (choose from green and red bell peppers, asparagus, broccoli, zucchini, yellow squash, mushrooms, green onions, sundried tomatoes soaked in olive oil [patted dry and chopped], *or* dry sundried tomatoes that have been rehydrated), *divided*

½ cup shredded cheddar cheese, *divided*

chopped chives, *divided*

1. Preheat the oven to 400°. Spray 6 6-ounce ramekins with nonstick cooking spray.
2. In a good-sized bowl, blend the eggs, half-and-half, salt, pepper, and thyme together. (A 4-cup measuring cup with a pouring spout is useful.) Set the mixture aside.
3. Fill each ramekin ¼ to ⅓ full with chopped vegetables.
4. Pour or spoon the egg mixture into the ramekins over the vegetables. Top with cheddar cheese and chives.
5. Bake for 20 to 30 minutes, or until set.

**Notes:** *You can multiply this recipe to serve more. Just keep the proportions the same.*

*If you have more bland veggies, be sure to add lots of thyme.*

*For cheese, Parmesan works well, especially with sun-dried tomatoes.*

Ever wonder what to do with a lot of leftover veggies? You don't have enough to make a full dish—just a little bit of each—but what you do have is a selection of fresh veggies! That happened to us one night when we added some last-minute guests to the list for breakfast in the morning—and voila, Garden-Baked Eggs were born!

This is a fun dish, filled with basic egg goodness, and easy to make your own.

This is one of my all-time favorite egg recipes. I even make it in my life as a retired innkeeper. It is a great way to make seafood part of your brunch table.

This recipe should be made only with real crabmeat, fresh from the ocean. No fake seafood for this Broad from the Pacific Northwest!

# Crab and Artichoke Egg Puff

JOYCE SCHULTE

*Serves 6*

*Prep Time: 30 minutes* ✿ *Baking Time: 30 minutes*

5 eggs

¼ cup flour

½ teaspoon baking powder

1 cup cottage cheese

2 cups grated Monterey Jack cheese

4 ounces shredded crabmeat

6 ounces chopped artichoke hearts

salt and pepper, to taste

6 drops Tabasco sauce

1. Preheat the oven to 350°. Spray 6 6-ounce ramekins with cooking spray.
2. In a medium bowl, combine the eggs, flour, and baking powder until well mixed.
3. Stir cottage cheese, grated Monterey Jack cheese, crabmeat, artichoke hearts, salt, pepper, and Tabasco sauce into the eggs. Mix well.
4. Divide the mixture equally among the ramekins.
5. Bake at 350° for approximately 30 minutes, or until golden brown.

**Notes:** *Top the egg puff with your favorite Hollandaise (or use the recipe on page 226) and a sprig of thyme or a roasted asparagus tip.*

*Serve with roasted asparagus and/or roasted bell peppers for a tasty light side.*

# Ham Baked Eggs

JOYCE SCHULTE

*Serves as many as needed*
*Prep Time: 15 to 20 minutes* 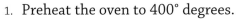 *Baking Time: 14 to 16 minutes*

**1 slice Black Forest ham, per serving**

**2 eggs, per serving**

**grated cheddar, Swiss, *or* Parmesan cheese**

**chopped parsley *or* chives, for garnish**

1. Preheat the oven to 400° degrees.
2. Grease 1 6-ounce ramekin per person. Or use a large greased muffin tin instead.
3. Lay 1 slice of ham on top of the ramekin and gently press it down into the well.
4. Crack 2 eggs into the well created by the ham.
5. Top the eggs with your choice of cheese.
6. Bake for 15 to 20 minutes or until the eggs are set.
7. Lift the baked ham and eggs from each ramekin and sprinkle with chopped parsley or chives.
8. Serve on a plate with roasted potatoes and fresh fruit.

Ham, cheddar cheese (we always use Tillamook, cause, hey, it's from Oregon, it's really good, and we live in the Pacific Northwest!), eggs, and ham. What's not to like?!

# Huevos Trifecta

KRISTIE ROSSET

*Serves 2*

*Prep Time: 30 minutes* ❧ *Cooking Time: 15 minutes*

¼ stick (2 tablespoons) butter

½ cup cream

4 eggs

dash of cayenne pepper

2 tablespoons grated cheddar cheese

1 large slice thinly sliced prosciutto, *divided* into 4 pieces

4 English muffins halves, toasted

dash of Mediterranean sea salt

4 sausage links, cooked

4 tomato slices

4 sprigs of fresh rosemary

1. In a skillet, melt butter over high heat. Immediately add the cream.
2. Slide the eggs into the butter and cream, being careful not to break them.
3. When the egg whites begin to set, flip the eggs over. Add a dash of cayenne pepper. Sprinkle with cheese.
4. Continue cooking until the egg yolks are done to your liking.
5. Place 1 piece of prosciutto atop each toasted English muffin half.
6. Slide 1 egg on top of each piece of prosciutto, along with some of the hot cream and butter.
7. Sprinkle Mediterranean sea salt on the eggs.
8. Place sausage links on the side. Garnish each plate with a slice of tomato and a rosemary sprig.

This is a funny name for a breakfast entrée. I am terrible at creating names, so when I introduced this entrée, I honestly did not know what to call it. When we served it to our inn guests for the first time and received raves, we asked them to suggest names.

Hot Springs is an historic horse-racing city with its popular Oaklawn Race Track. Many of our guests had attended the races on the day before we served this breakfast dish. When one guest suggested the name, "Huevos Trifecta," we knew we had a winner.

"Huevos"="eggs," in Spanish. "Trifecta," a wagering term at the races, stands for the three layers in this dish—English muffin, prosciutto, and eggs.

# Basil and Tomato Egg Scramble

YVONNE MARTIN

*6 servings*
*Prep Time: 15 minutes*  *Cooking Time: 10 minutes*

**12 eggs**

**1 cup milk**

**⅓ cup sour cream**

**½ teaspoon salt**

**½ teaspoon pepper**

**8 leaves fresh basil, *or*
1 teaspoon dried basil**

**2 tablespoons chopped
chives, *or* spring onions**

**¼ stick (2 tablespoons)
butter, *or* olive oil**

**½ cup halved
cherry tomatoes**

**½ cup crumbled feta
cheese, *divided***

1. In a good-sized bowl, beat the eggs, milk, sour cream, salt, and pepper together.
2. If you're using fresh basil, cut it into fine strips. Mix the basil and chives into the egg batter.
3. Melt the butter in a large skillet over medium heat. Pour in the egg batter and cook, stirring gently, until curds start to form.
4. Fold in the cherry tomatoes and half the feta cheese.
5. Continue cooking until the egg curds are almost set. Don't cook until they're totally dry; the eggs will continue to cook after they're removed from the heat.
6. Sprinkle the scramble with the remaining feta cheese. Serve immediately.

# Tomatoes Benedict

YVONNE MARTIN

*Serves 6*
*Prep Time: 15 minutes* ❧ *Baking Time: 25 to 30 minutes*

about 6 large fresh
plum tomatoes

¼ cup mayonnaise

2 teaspoons dried basil

1½ cups shredded
cheddar cheese

½ cup shredded Asiago,
*or* Parmesan, cheese

12 eggs

6 English muffins

chopped fresh parsley,
for garnish

1. Preheat the oven to 350°. Spray a 9-inch pie plate with non-stick cooking spray.
2. Dice the plum tomatoes into ½-inch cubes. Drain off any excess liquid.
3. In a bowl, combine the cubed tomatoes with the mayonnaise, basil, cheddar, and Asiago cheeses.
4. Pour the mixture into the pie plate. Bake for about 25 to 30 minutes, until the top is golden brown.
5. While tomatoes are baking, poach the eggs. Split the English muffins and toast them.
6. Place 2 toasted muffin halves on each plate. Divide the tomato mixture between the muffins. Top each muffin half with a poached egg. Sprinkle each egg with fresh parsley and serve.

This is a versatile side dish that can be used several different ways. In this recipe, the Benedict is served under poached eggs. Sometimes we serve it over scrambled eggs. And we've even served it as a hot appetizer dish with crostini.

Our Smoked Salmon Eggs Benedict is an example of choosing the best ingredients and then putting them together in such a way that you have an exceptional outcome. We are very fortunate in Seattle to have access to amazing Alaskan smoked salmon. This certainly contributes to making a wonderful Benedict breakfast.

# Smoked Salmon Eggs Benedict

JOYCE SCHULTE

*Serves 4*

*Prep time: 25 minutes (without the Hollandaise)* ❧ *Cooking time: 10 to 15 minutes*

4 large slices, *or* 8 small slices, of your favorite artisan bread such as sourdough *or* ciabatta

2 tablespoons olive oil

4 teaspoons white vinegar, *divided*

8 eggs

8 slices smoked salmon (we prefer Alaskan)

1 cup Hollandaise sauce (see recipe page 226)

sprinkle of paprika, *or* fresh thyme

1. Preheat the oven to 400°.
2. Using a pastry brush, lightly coat both sides of the slices of bread with olive oil. Lay them on a baking sheet and place in the oven to toast. Turn after 5 minutes, cooking until crispy.
3. Prepare the Hollandaise sauce according to the recipe on page 226.
4. Poach 4 eggs at a time in a 10-inch skillet. To poach, fill the skillet ⅔ full of water, add half the vinegar, and bring to a boil over medium-high heat.
5. Crack each egg into a small bowl or ramekin, being careful not to break the yolk. When the water is boiling, slip 4 eggs into the pan.
6. Cook until the yolks are done to your liking, approximately 4 minutes. Remove each egg with a slotted spoon, draining off any water.
7. Top the larger slices of bread with 2 poached eggs each. Top the smaller slices with 1 egg each.
8. Repeat Steps 4 through 7 with the remaining 4 eggs.
9. Place a slice of smoked salmon on top of each egg.
10. Drizzle each serving of two eggs with ¼ cup Hollandaise sauce.
11. Lightly dust paprika or fresh thyme on top to add both a pop of color and flavor that mixes well with the salmon and Hollandaise.

While on a business retreat in Santa Fe, New Mexico, the 8 Broads saw the movie "Chef." This movie elevated grilled cheese sandwiches to an art form, and I've been serving grilled cheese sandwiches ever since in various iterations: for breakfast, for lunch, for dinner. For guests in my inn, the grilled cheese sandwich is sublime. Try this version, and then create your own unique grilled cheese.

This sandwich is such as big hit at Lookout Point that the plates usually come back totally clean! In Arkansas, bacon makes just about every meal taste better; however, you can substitute turkey bacon or skip the meat completely.

# Grilled Cheese Bacon-Avocado-Tomato Sandwich (aka "Cheese & BAT")

KRISTIE ROSSET

*Serves 4*
*Prep time: 40 minutes (less if you're using pre-cooked bacon)*
*Griddle Time: 6 to 8 minutes*

2 tablespoons mayonnaise, *divided*

8 slices artisan bread

8 slices cheese (your choice of Pepper Jack, Colby, cheddar, or Provolone), *divided*

8 slices bacon, cooked, *divided*

2 tomatoes, thinly sliced, *divided*

2 avocados, cut into ¼-inch-thick slices, *divided*

2 teaspoons Dijon mustard, *divided*

butter, softened to room temperature

1. Spread ½ tablespoon of mayonnaise on one slice of bread.
2. Then top with one slice of cheese, 2 pieces of bacon, 2 or 3 slices of tomato (depending on the circumference), and 4 slices of avocado.
3. Top with one remaining slice of cheese.
4. Spread ½ teaspoon Dijon mustard on the 2nd slice of bread and close the sandwich.
5. Repeat for the remaining 3 sandwiches.
6. Thickly spread the softened butter on the outside of one side of each sandwich.
7. Preheat the griddle to 325°.
8. Place the sandwiches butter-side down on the griddle.
9. Spread butter on the top side of each sandwich while they are cooking.
10. Slowly griddle the sandwiches until the bread is golden brown and the cheese begins to melt, about 4 minutes.
11. When ready, flip the sandwiches and continue to cook the second side until it's golden brown.
12. Remove from the griddle and serve.

# Smoked Salmon Avocado Toast

JOYCE SCHULTE

*Makes 4 toasts or 2 sandwiches*
*Prep Time: 15 to 20 minutes*

1 large avocado

1 tablespoon lime juice

1 teaspoon cumin

salt, to taste, *optional*

4 slices whole-grain
artisan bread

4 to 6 ounces smoked
salmon (slices work best)

arugula, *or* a mix
of spicy greens, *or*
radishes *or* cucumbers

1. Peel and chop the avocado into a medium bowl. Mash with a fork or large spoon till chunky.
2. Add the lime juice, and cumin. Mash a bit more till the mixture is just slightly chunky. Add salt if desired.
3. Toast 4 slices of bread.
4. Spread a layer of the avocado mixture on each piece of bread.
5. Top each with 1 to 1½ ounces of salmon.
6. Top with arugula, greens, or thinly sliced radishes or cucumbers.
7. Serve immediately.

**Note:** *This recipe is for four toasts or two sandwiches and can be easily multiplied by the number of people you are serving.*

# Potato Veggie Pancakes

DANIELLE HANSCOM

*Serves 8 (Makes 14 to 16 pancakes)*
*Prep Time: 15 to 20 minutes* *Griddle Time: 10 to 15 minutes*

4 large potatoes

¼ cup diced onion

¼ cup diced red bell peppers

¼ cup julienned zucchini, *or* yellow squash

½ cup coarsely chopped mushrooms

¼ cup sliced leeks, *or* scallions

2 tablespoons chopped fresh parsley

2 tablespoons flour

3 large eggs, beaten

2 tablespoons water

¼ stick (2 tablespoons) butter, melted

¼ cup grated sharp cheddar cheese, *optional*

½ teaspoon salt

⅛ teaspoon freshly ground pepper

oil *or* butter, for the griddle

1. Cook and chill the potatoes. (This can be done the day before.)
2. Prepare the onions, peppers, zucchini, mushrooms, leeks, and parsley.
3. Preheat a griddle or frying pan. Grease it with some oil or butter or a combination of both.
4. Peel and grate the potatoes into a good-sized bowl with a coarse grater.
5. Add the prepared vegetables, flour, eggs, water, melted butter, cheese, salt, and pepper. Mix gently with a spoon or spatula until combined. You don't want the potatoes to lose their shredded shape!
6. Using a medium-sized ice cream scoop that holds about ¼ cup, drop the mixture onto a hot griddle. Do not pack or form the pancakes. They're better if they're somewhat loosely connected. Press only enough to shape and hold them together.
7. Fry until golden brown, flipping once. Serve hot.

*These pancakes are one of our most popular and easy-to-make sides. Feel free to substitute veggies in and out; the recipe works with all of them. Use a cookie dipper to portion them onto a hot griddle or pan.*

# Southwest Sausage Strata

YVONNE MARTIN

*Serves 12*

*Prep Time: 30 minutes* ❧ *Standing Time: 30 minutes* ❧ *Baking Time: 45 minutes*

1 pound ground sausage (your choice of chorizo, turkey, hot *or* mild Italian)

4 small cans chopped green chilies, drained

8 small tortillas, corn *or* wheat, cut in ½-inch-wide strips, *divided*

2 cups shredded cheddar cheese, *divided*

14-ounce can diced tomatoes, drained

12 eggs

1½ cups milk

½ teaspoon salt

½ teaspoon black pepper

2 cloves chopped garlic

1 teaspoon ground cumin

2 teaspoons dried onion flakes

2 cups sour cream

2 cups salsa

chopped cilantro for garnish, *optional*

1. Fry the sausage, crumbling it into small pieces. Drain off the drippings and discard them.
2. Preheat the oven to 350°. Grease either a 9- x 13-inch baking dish or 2 9-inch, deep-dish pie plates.
3. Spread all of the chopped chilies in the bottom of the prepared large baking dish, or divide them between the two pie plates.
4. Layer with half the tortillas, then half the sausage, and then half the cheese. Repeat the layers. Arrange the diced tomatoes on top.
5. In a good-sized bowl, beat the eggs, milk, salt, pepper, garlic, cumin, and onion flakes together.
6. Pour carefully over the tortilla mix. Allow to sit for at least 30 minutes before baking to allow the tortillas to absorb the liquid.
7. Bake uncovered for about 45 minutes, or until a knife inserted in the center comes out clean.
8. Serve with sour cream, salsa, and chopped cilantro.

This recipe can be assembled the night before you want to serve it. Refrigerate it, and then bake it in the morning, after bringing it to room temperature for about 30 minutes.

# Black Bean and Tortilla Strata

KRISTIE ROSSET

*Serves 12*
*Prep Time: 40 minutes* ❧ *Chilling Time: 12 hours, or overnight*
*Baking Time: 65 minutes*

1 cup salsa, your choice of mild to medium

1 cup cooked black beans, rinsed and drained

12 corn tortillas, cut into 1-inch-wide strips, *divided*

1½ cups shredded Monterey Jack cheese, *divided*

1 cup sour cream

1 cup milk

6 large eggs, beaten

¼ cup sliced green onions

¼ cup diced green chilies, drained

1 teaspoon salt

1 tablespoon fresh cilantro

1 tablespoon dried onion flakes

sour cream

picante sauce

1. Mix salsa and black beans together in a bowl.
2. In a greased 9- x 13-inch baking dish, layer ⅓ of the tortilla strips on the bottom.
3. Spread half the bean/salsa mix over the tortilla strips.
4. Scatter half the cheese over the beans and salsa.
5. Repeat the layers, using half of the remaining tortilla strips, all of the bean/salsa mix, and half the remaining cheese. (Place the remaining cheese in a covered container and refrigerate until needed in the morning.)
6. Layer the remaining tortilla strips on top.
7. In a good-sized bowl, blend together the sour cream, milk, eggs, green onions, green chilies, salt, cilantro, and onion flakes. Pour over the tortilla layers.
8. Cover with foil and refrigerate for 12 hours or overnight.
9. In the morning, preheat the oven to 375°. Bake covered for 45 minutes. Uncover and sprinkle with the remaining cheese.

10. Bake uncovered for another 15 to 20 minutes, until the strata appears set and the cheese is bubbly.
11. Serve with sour cream and picante sauce.

Who doesn't like a great breakfast casserole that you can prepare the night before serving, and then just pop it into the oven the next morning? Plus the black beans make me feel like I'm eating a bit healthier.

# Breakfast Burrito

LYNNETTE SCOFIELD

*Serves 4*

*Prep time: 15 minutes ✂ Cook time: 10 minutes*

8 eggs

8 tablespoons cream cheese, softened to room temperature

1 teaspoon fresh parsley, *or* cilantro

1 teaspoon dried dill

4 large tortillas, flour, *or* spinach if you want to add a bit of color and extra flavor

1⅓ cups shredded cheese, such as pepper *or* Monterey Jack, *or* cheddar

½ cup diced tomatoes

½ cup green chilies

½ cup cooked black beans

1. Whisk the eggs in a bowl, and then scramble them in a skillet until they are just cooked but still moist. (I prefer to use club soda instead of milk if I add any liquid to the eggs.)
2. Mix the parsley and dill with the cream cheese.
3. Preheat the oven to 300°. Lay the tortillas flat on a foil-lined baking sheet. Place them in the oven for about 3 minutes until they're warm.
4. Spread 2 tablespoons of the herbed cream cheese on each tortilla, then top with ¼ of the scrambled eggs on each tortilla.
5. Next comes a layer of your favorite shredded cheese. Sprinkle about ⅓ cup on each tortilla.
6. Return the tortillas to the oven for 3 minutes to warm slightly.
7. Remove from the oven. Top each tortilla with about 2 tablespoons of each remaining topping.
8. Fold the sides of each tortilla toward its middle. Then roll from one end to the other.
9. Wrap in parchment paper that has been cut on the diagonal. Secure with fun toothpicks.
10. We serve these with home fries, homemade pepper jelly and a bit of sour cream.

**Note:** *If you wish, substitute other ingredients for the tomatoes, chilies and beans, such as: diced onions, sautéed mushrooms, cooked sausage or chorizo, or salsa. Two to three tablespoons of each selection will be plenty to fill the burrito.*

This is the easiest and tastiest breakfast that will use (almost!) anything you might have in the fridge—tomatoes, peppers, salsa, cream cheese, fresh herbs, cheddar, sausage. You name it, it will work!

# Mushroom Crepes with Shiitake & Spinach Sauce

DEBBIE MOSIMANN

*Makes 8 to 10 crepes*
*Prep Time: 25 minutes  ✣  Cooking Time: 15 minutes*

**For the Crepes:**

1 cup flour

¼ teaspoon salt

2 eggs, beaten

½ cup milk

½ cup water

¼ stick (2 tablespoons) butter, melted

**To make the Crepes:**

1. Measure the flour and salt into a bowl.
2. Add the eggs, milk, water, and butter. Whisk until smooth.
3. Heat a non-stick 9-inch skillet until hot. Then brush the pan with oil or additional butter.
4. Pour ¼ cup batter into the skillet. Immediately tilt the pan to coat the bottom with the batter.
5. Cook 1 minute before flipping the crepe to the other side.
6. Cook until it loses its glossy shine—less than a minute—then remove it to a plate. Repeat with the rest of the batter.

**Note:** *You can make the unfilled crepes, a day ahead of when you want to serve them. Just refrigerate them until you need them.*

**For the Filling and Sauce:**

1 pound mixed mushrooms (shiitake, oyster, crimini, or other favorites)

¼ onion, finely chopped

3 tablespoons butter

1 teaspoon prepared mustard

2 tablespoons flour

½ cup white wine

2 cups roughly chopped baby spinach

2 tablespoons brandy

½ cup stock (use vegetable if serving vegetarians; otherwise, use chicken)

½ teaspoon salt

¼ teaspoon pepper

1 stalk thyme, leaves only, *or* about ¼ teaspoon dried thyme

½ cup whipping cream

**To make the Filling and Sauce:**

1. Chop and dice the mushrooms and onions.
2. Heat the butter in a skillet. Sauté the mushrooms and onions until soft. Stir in the mustard.
3. Stir in the flour and allow the mixture to brown slightly.
4. Add the white wine, stirring until smooth.
5. Add the spinach leaves and the brandy. Add the stock and stir until the mixture is smooth.
6. Add the salt, pepper, thyme, and, lastly, the whipping cream. Stir until well mixed and heated through, but not boiling.
7. Lay a crepe on a plate. Spoon about ¼ cup of the mushroom spinach mixture onto the crepe, just enough to cover it.
8. Fold the crepe in half and then in half again. Place on a serving plate. Keep the filled crepe warm as you make the rest of the crepes.
9. Serve immediately with salad.

If you've never made crepes, it's much easier than it sounds. You can use the basic crepe recipe and directions with any type of filling that you prefer, from sweet to savory. This savory recipe is full of great flavors!

# Shakshouka Flatbread

DEBBIE MOSIMANN

*Serves*
*Dough Prep Time: 1 hour, including the rising time* ✂ *Shakshouka Prep Time: 20 minutes*
*Baking Time: 18 to 20 minutes*

## For the Dough:

1¼ cups flour

¼ cup semolina flour

1 teaspoon salt

1 teaspoon instant dry yeast

½ cup warm water

1 tablespoon oil

## To make the Dough:

1. Measure the flours, salt, and yeast into a good-sized bowl.
2. Gradually add the warm water. Immediately add the oil.
3. Pull the dough together into a ball with a mixing spoon. If it is too dry to hold together, add 1 teaspoon of water at a time until the dough pulls together and away from the sides of the bowl.
4. On a lightly floured surface knead the dough until smooth, about 1 minute. Put the ball of dough back in the bowl, cover it, and allow it to rise in a warm place until double in size, about 45 minutes.
5. While the dough is rising, make the Shakshouka.

With such a bold name, you expect a boldly flavored dish. You will not be disappointed! Originating in northern Africa, this dish showcases the spices for which the region is known. The eggs on top help to mellow it out and allow it to be a meal in itself. Play with the spices until you find the level you love.

### For the Shakshouka

2 tablespoons oil

¾ teaspoon ground cumin

½ teaspoon paprika (a sweet Hungarian smoked paprika is especially good)

¼ teaspoon coriander

pinch of saffron

½ medium onion, diced

1 clove garlic, crushed

1 medium red bell pepper, diced

3 medium tomatoes, diced

4 large eggs

parsley to garnish

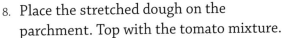

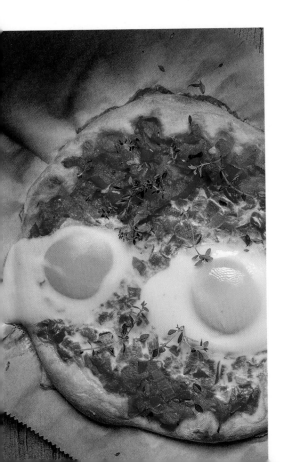

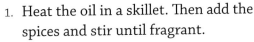

1. Heat the oil in a skillet. Then add the spices and stir until fragrant.
2. Add the onion and garlic. Sauté for 30 seconds.
3. Add the pepper and tomatoes. Cook over medium heat, stirring as needed until most of the moisture is gone, about 15 minutes. The tomatoes will dissolve and the peppers will be very tender.
4. Remove from the stove. This step can be done up to 2 days ahead and stored in the refrigerator.
5. When you're ready to serve the meal, preheat the oven to 450°.
6. Line a baking sheet with parchment.
7. When the dough has doubled in size, lightly grease your hands, remove the dough from the bowl, then stretch and roll it into a very thin, oblong shape. Or cut it in half and create 2 smaller thin, oblong shapes.
8. Place the stretched dough on the parchment. Top with the tomato mixture.
9. Place in the preheated oven. Bake for 8 to 10 minutes.
10. Meanwhile, crack the eggs into a bowl. When the flatbread is puffed but not yet brown, pull the oven rack forward. Gently pour one egg after the other onto the tomato mixture, spreading them evenly over the bread, but without breaking the yolks.
11. Return the bread and eggs to the oven. Bake for another 10 minutes. Do not overbake! You want the eggs to be soft in the middle.
12. Remove from the oven. Sprinkle with chopped parsley and serve immediately.

# Mushroom Sausage Bread Pudding

DEBBIE MOSIMANN

*Serves 8*
*Prep Time: 15 to 20 minutes ❧ Chilling Time: 1 to 12 hours or overnight*
*Standing Time: 30 minutes ❧ Baking Time: 45 to 60 minutes*

5 to 6 cups day-old bread, cubed

1 pound sausage, removed from its casing

¼ stick (2 tablespoons) butter

12 ounces fresh mushrooms (your choice of variety), sliced thin

3 tablespoons flour

2½ cups milk, *divided*

½ teaspoon dry mustard

6 eggs

½ teaspoon salt

pepper, to taste

½ cup grated Emmentaler cheese

½ cup grated Gruyère cheese

1. Spray a 9- x 13-inch baking dish with nonstick cooking spray. Spread the cubed bread evenly in the pan. Set it aside.
2. In a skillet, brown the sausage, crumbling as you go. Remove the sausage and set it aside.
3. Using the same skillet, melt the butter, then add the sliced mushrooms. Sauté them until they're tender and slightly brown.
4. Turn off the heat. Add the flour, mixing it in well.
5. Pour in 1 cup of the milk a little at a time, stirring constantly to make a creamy mushroom sauce. Set it aside.
6. In a bowl, mix the 1½ cups milk, mustard, eggs, salt, and pepper until well blended.
7. Evenly distribute the cooked sausage over top of the bread.
8. Pour the egg mixture over the sausage and bread.
9. Mix the grated cheeses into the cooled mushroom sauce. Then spread the sauce over the sausage layer.
10. Cover and refrigerate overnight, or for a minimum of 1 hour.

11. When you're ready to bake the bread pudding, remove it from the refrigerator, take off the cover, and allow the dish to stand for 30 minutes to lose some of its chill.
12. Preheat the oven to 350°.
13. Bake the sausage soufflé for 45 to 60 minutes, or until it puffs a bit and a toothpick inserted into the center comes out clean.

**Notes:** *We think a mild salt-and-pepper sausage is best for this recipe.*

*I like to grate the cheeses ahead of when I need them and then freeze them so I have them for quick use.*

Some dishes just rise to the top as perennial favorites. This is hands down, far and away, my family's favorite breakfast dish. As our daughters married and left home, this was the recipe they made sure to take with them so they could have it ready for company.

# Kiss My Grits!

ELLEN GUTMAN CHENAUX

*Serves 8*
*Prep and Cooking Time for the Grits: 45 minutes  ✇  Additional Prep Time: 10 minutes*
*Baking Time: 60 minutes for a large pan; 45 minutes for individual dishes*

**For the Grits:**

4½ cups water

1 cup stone-ground yellow grits

1 teaspoon salt

¼ stick (2 tablespoons) unsalted butter

**For the Breakfast Entrée:**

½ pound sweet Italian turkey sausage, squeezed out of its casing

½ pound hot Italian turkey sausage, squeezed out of its casing

1 large onion, chopped

half a stick (4 tablespoons) unsalted butter, cut into chunks

2 eggs, lightly beaten

2 cups grated cheddar, *or* Parmesan, cheese

¼ cup minced fresh parsley, *or* basil

**To make the Grits:**

1. Mix the water, grits, salt, and butter in a large saucepan or pot. Bring to a boil over medium heat.
2. Reduce the heat to low. Cover and simmer for 45 minutes or until thick. If the grits become too thick, add more water.

**To make the Breakfast Entrée:**

1. Preheat the oven to 400°. Grease a 9- x 13-inch baking pan, or eight 6- or 8-inch ramekins.
2. Sauté the sausage in a skillet, breaking it into small pieces. Using a slotted spoon, remove the sausage from the pan and place it in a good-sized bowl.
3. Sauté the onion in the fat from the sausage. Drain. Add the onion to the sausage.
4. Add the butter, eggs, cheese, and parsley or basil to the grits. Stir together well.
5. Combine the grits mixture with the sausage and onions.
6. Pour into the prepared pan or individual ramekins. At this point, you can refrigerate the entree for up to 2 days before baking. It also freezes well.
7. When ready to serve, bake at 400° for 1 hour (or 45 minutes if using ramekins), or until brown.

On my first trip to Charleston, I went to a cooking store and asked the owner for the secret to making great grits. I was told to use Carolina Plantation Stone Ground Grits. And then this recipe just took off from there and became a national savory breakfast contest winner!

# Mini Corn Cakes

YVONNE MARTIN

*Serves 12 to 16 (approximately 3 mini cakes per person)*
*Prep Time: 20 minutes* ❧ *Griddle Time: 6 to 8 minutes*

1¾ cups milk

2 tablespoons lemon juice

1½ cups flour

1½ teaspoons baking soda

1½ tablespoons sugar

¾ teaspoon salt

2 eggs

3 tablespoons melted butter

4 cups fresh *or* frozen corn kernels

½ cup very finely diced red bell pepper

3 tablespoons chopped fresh parsley

2 tablespoons chopped fresh chives
*or* 2 teaspoons dried chives

½ teaspoon pepper

sour cream

1. Preheat the griddle; then grease it.
2. Pour the milk into a small bowl. Stir in the lemon juice. Let the mixture stand for several minutes so the juice can sour the milk.
3. Combine the flour, baking soda, sugar, and salt in a mixing bowl. Mix with a fork.
4. In a separate large bowl, whisk together the soured milk, eggs, and melted butter.
5. Add the dry ingredients to the liquids. Stir well.
6. Mix in the corn, red bell pepper, parsley, chives, and pepper.
7. Drop by generous tablespoons onto a hot griddle. Cook until done on both sides.
8. Serve warm with a dollop of sour cream.

*These make a great side dish for breakfast or brunch.*
*We've also served them as appetizers with dinner.*

# Spinach Brownies

ELLEN GUTMAN CHENAUX

*Serves 12*
*Prep Time: 15 minutes* ❧ *Baking Time: 35 to 40 minutes*

half a stick (4 tablespoons) unsalted butter

2 10-ounce packages chopped frozen spinach, thawed and squeezed to remove moisture

3 eggs

1 cup milk

1 cup flour

1 teaspoon salt

1 teaspoon baking powder

1 pound grated, aged white cheddar cheese

1. Preheat the oven to 350°. Grease a 9- x 13-inch baking dish.
2. Melt the butter in the baking dish.
3. Thaw the spinach and drain it well. Squeeze the spinach to remove as much moisture as possible. Set it aside.
4. In a good-sized mixing bowl, beat the eggs and add the milk.
5. In a separate bowl, mix the flour, salt, and baking powder together. Add to the egg/milk mixture.
6. Stir in the cheese and spinach. Mix well. Spoon the mixture into the baking dish.
7. Bake at 350° for 35 to 45 minutes, until the top is lightly brown. (If the mixture is chilled, bake for 50 to 60 minutes.)
8. Cool slightly before cutting into squares or triangles.

*This is really a crustless spinach quiche, but calling it "brownies" is much more fun!*
*See them in the photo on page 162.*

# Side Dishes

## Sidekicks

# Glazed Bacon

KRISTIE ROSSET

*Serves 4*
*Prep Time: 10 minutes* ✽ *Baking Time: 15 to 20 minutes*

**1 pound thick-sliced bacon**

**¼ cup Dijon mustard**

**½ cup brown sugar,
lightly packed**

**Notes:** *Be careful not to overcook the bacon with the glaze, or the glaze will harden and stick to your teeth.*

*To spice it up a bit, sprinkle the brown sugar with dried red pepper flakes.*

1. Preheat the oven to 375°.
2. Lay bacon strips on a foil-lined rimmed baking sheet (15 x 10 x 1-inch).
3. Bake until about half-cooked.
4. Remove the pan from the oven. Brush each bacon slice with Dijon mustard. Sprinkle with brown sugar.
5. Bake for approximately 15 more minutes, or until the bacon is as crisp as you like it.
6. Remove the bacon to serving plates and keep it warm until you're ready to serve.

*My oh my, requests for seconds abound whenever I serve glazed bacon. It's simply divine, and in the South, we sure do like bacon.*

# Apple Sausage Bake

KATHRYN WHITE
SERVES 12

*Prep Time: 15 minutes* ❧ *Baking Time: 60 minutes*

⅓ cup finely chopped onions

oil, to sauté onions

3 pounds sausage of your choice, squeezed out of its casing

2¼ cups herbed bread stuffing

3 eggs, lightly beaten

¾ cup milk

1 finely diced large apple

½ teaspoon dried sage

salt and pepper, to taste

1. Preheat the oven to 350°.
2. Sauté the onions in a small amount of oil in a skillet over low heat until they're translucent.
3. Place the loose sausage meat in a large bowl. Add the onions, stuffing, eggs, milk, apple, and seasonings. Mix together until blended well.
4. Line a baking sheet with quick release aluminum foil (or use regular foil and spray it lightly with oil).
5. Form the sausage mixture into 3 log-like shapes. Place them on the baking sheet.
6. Bake for 55 minutes.
7. Slice to serve.

Apples and sausage just go together perfectly. If you have a house full of guests, create the mixture and form the round "log" the night before. Refrigerate it overnight, then allow it to sit on the counter for about 20 minutes to take the chill off before baking it in the morning.

# Ham, Apple, and Goat Cheese Breakfast Toast

KATHRYN WHITE

*Serves 8*
*Prep Time: 12 to 15 minutes* ✣ *Baking Time: 15 minutes*

8 slices Saloio bread
*or* other dense bread

½ cup apple
butter, *divided*

½ pound thinly
sliced ham, *or*
prosciutto, *divided*

2 Granny Smith apples,
peeled, cored, and
thinly sliced, *divided*

8 ounces goat
cheese, *divided*

pepper, to taste, *optional*

finely chopped fresh
parsley for garnish

1. Preheat the oven to 375°.
2. Heat a griddle with a light covering of olive oil.
3. Place the 8 slices of bread on the griddle. Toast each side, and place on a baking sheet.
4. Spread apple butter on one side of each slice of bread. Place a slice of ham on top of the apple butter, folding as necessary.
5. Position apple slices on top of the ham slices, and then add slices of goat cheese over the apples. Add freshly ground pepper on the cheese, if desired.
6. Bake in the oven for about 15 minutes or until the cheese melts.
7. Remove from the oven and sprinkle chopped parsley over the tops of the toast.
8. Serve with scrambled eggs.

I attended a cooking class where these ingredients were to be served on a crepe. Well, I wanted a sturdier base, so I played around and came up with this version. Enjoy!

# Sweet Potato Hash

KATHRYN WHITE

*Serves 8*
*Prep Time: 15 to 20 minutes* ❧ *Cooking Time: 15 minutes*

2 medium sweet potatoes
(about 1½ pounds), peeled
and diced into ½-inch cubes

2 tablespoons olive oil

1 pound ground sausage,
your choice of flavors

½ cup diced celery

½ chopped onion

1 Granny Smith apple,
peeled, cored, and diced

½ teaspoon ground sage

salt and freshly ground pepper

1. In a saucepan, boil enough water to cover the diced sweet potatoes. Drop the sweet potatoes into the water and cook until barely tender, about 4 to 5 minutes. Drain and set aside.
2. In a large skillet, heat the olive oil. Stir in the sausage. Brown until thoroughly cooked and crumbled, about 10 minutes. Remove the sausage with a slotted spoon. Drain it on paper towels to remove the grease.
3. Add the celery and onion to the same skillet. Cook in the drippings until just tender.
4. Add the apples. Cook for another 3 to 4 minutes.
5. Add the cooked sweet potatoes and sausage to the mixture.
6. Season with sage, and salt and pepper to taste.
7. Use as a side to scrambled eggs. Or poach or fry eggs and place them on top of the hash.

*We love sweet potatoes! This is a yummy side for eggs.
For vegetarians, omit the sausage.*

# Neapolitan Potatoes

YVONNE MARTIN

*Serves 12*
*Prep Time: 20 minutes* ❧ *Baking Time: 1¼ hours*

about 12 medium-size red,
*or* Yukon Gold potatoes

14-ounce can diced
tomatoes, drained

3 cloves garlic, finely chopped

½ cup olive oil

2 tablespoons dried basil

1. Preheat the oven to 375°. Spray a 9- x 13-inch baking pan with nonstick coating.
2. Wash and dry the potatoes. Cut each potato in half lengthwise, then in half lengthwise again, then in half through the middle, to yield 8 pieces per potato.
3. In a good-sized bowl, combine the tomatoes, garlic, olive oil, and basil. Then add the potatoes and toss together.
4. Pour the potatoes into the greased baking dish. Cover with foil.
5. Bake at 375° for about 45 minutes.
6. Remove the foil and bake for an additional 30 minutes, or until the potatoes are soft when pierced with a fork.

*Not your usual roasted potato dish, this recipe is colorful and interesting on a buffet table. Plus who doesn't love garlic and tomato anything?*

# Have you tried these?

Strawberry Cornmeal Muffins, page 53

Caramel Peach Bread Pudding, page 116

Mediterranean Quiche, page 140

Ray's Strawberry Soup, page 37

# Potato Galette

KATHRYN WHITE

*Serves 4 to 6*
*Prep Time: 10 minutes ❧ Baking Time: 15 to 20 minutes*

3 medium Yukon Gold
potatoes (about one pound)

2 to 3 tablespoons olive oil

1 teaspoon
Herbes de Provence

1 or 2 tomatoes, sliced

freshly ground pepper
and salt, to taste

chopped fresh parsley

1. Preheat the oven to 375°. Line a baking sheet with parchment paper, or use Silpat or your favorite non-stick baking mat. If you're using parchment paper, brush lightly with olive oil.
2. Scrub the potatoes clean, and using a mandolin, slice the potatoes about ⅛-inch thick.
3. Arrange the potatoes on the prepared baking sheet in a spiral to make 4 to 6 rounds. (One round serves one person.)
4. Brush the potatoes with olive oil. Place a slice of tomato on each round group of potatoes.
5. Sprinkle with Herbes de Provence, salt and pepper to taste.
6. Bake for approximately 15 to 20 minutes. The time will vary depending upon how thick the potato slices are. Remove from the oven when the edges are brown and the potatoes are cooked through.
7. Garnish with chopped fresh parsley and serve immediately.

## Variations:

*You can use fresh thyme, rosemary, or parsley instead of Herbes de Provence.*

*You can also add your favorite grated cheese to the potatoes. Parmigiano Reggiano and Gruyere are both good choices.*

*Use red potatoes instead of Yukon Golds.*

*Instead of, or in addition to, tomatoes, top the galette with chopped spinach, sliced zucchini or asparagus pieces. Add a poached egg to the top, and breakfast is ready!*

Potatoes are a perfect complement to any brunch or breakfast menu. Instead of home fries, try a free-form galette for a change. It's easily served as a side. Or you can add vegetables and a poached egg in layers on top of the potatoes and serve it as an entrée.

# Creamy Polenta or Grits

KATHRYN WHITE

*Serves 8*
*Prep Time: 10 to 15 minutes* ❧ *Cooking Time: 45 minutes*

3 cups water

1 cup uncooked polenta (labeled "traditional" and not "quick") *or* stone-ground grits

⅓ cup heavy cream

half a stick (4 tablespoons) butter, cut into chunks

2 cups (8 ounces) grated sharp cheddar cheese

2 eggs, lightly beaten

1 teaspoon salt

½ teaspoon freshly ground black pepper

1 tablespoon chopped fresh parsley

1. Boil the water in a large pot. Add the polenta very slowly in a steady stream. Stir constantly while doing so, and for several minutes following to avoid lumps.
2. Lower the heat and cook the polenta for 30 minutes. It will thicken as it cooks.
3. Add the heavy cream, butter, grated cheese, and eggs. Stir until blended. Add salt, pepper, and parsley and cook for another 5 minutes.
4. Remove from the heat and serve immediately as a side to eggs and bacon.

## Variations:

*After Step 1, pour the mixture into a 9- x 13-inch baking pan and cool. Cover and refrigerate. Instead of using English muffins as a base for Eggs Benedict, slice the polenta, place it on a baking sheet, and warm it in a 325° oven for 10 to 15 minutes. Or sauté it in a skillet (using butter or olive oil) over medium heat for 3 to 4 minutes on each side.*

*Or slice the polenta and layer it with fresh spinach, tomatoes, and/or cheese, topped with poached eggs, for a gluten-free breakfast entrée.*

*Use chopped green onions or scallions to garnish polenta with a bit of zip.*

Polenta and grits are both made from ground corn. If you're from the North, it's "polenta"; from the South, it's "grits."

Recipes are as varied as there are grandmothers. Some insist on using milk; some only water. Some make it for breakfast only; others for three meals a day.

I have good success with stone-ground grits from Anson Mills, Geechie Boy Mill, and Carolina Plantation Rice.

# Parmesan Heirloom Cherry Tomatoes

DEBBIE MOSIMANN

*Serves 6*

*Prep Time: 10 minutes* 🌿 *Baking Time: 15 minutes*

2 pints heirloom cherry tomatoes, red and yellow

½ cup panko bread crumbs

¼ cup coarsely grated Parmesan cheese

cracked black pepper, to taste

sea salt, to taste

¼ cup chopped fresh herbs—any combination of basil, parsley, and chives

2 tablespoons oil to drizzle

1. Preheat the oven to 375°.
2. Cut the cherry tomatoes in half lengthwise.
3. In a bowl, toss the tomatoes with the panko, Parmesan, cracked pepper, salt, and herbs.
4. Spoon into 6 lightly greased 4-inch ramekins. Drizzle with oil.
5. Bake at 375° until a slight brown shows on some of the tomatoes, about 15 minutes.
6. Serve hot.

This makes a beautiful side dish for dinner as well as breakfast. It's bright with a bit of crunch and such bold flavors.

Whoever realized that you could have veggies for breakfast and love them so? This is more of a process than a recipe, because you can use whatever veggies you have on hand. I love the color of beets and carrots, but mix and match as you please. Baby pattypan squash look especially appealing. This makes an excellent side at breakfast, or serve it with fried eggs on top.

# Roasted Fall Root Vegetables

DEBBIE MOSIMANN

*Serves 6*

*Prep Time: 15 minutes* ❧ *Baking Time: 15 to 20 minutes*

3 red-skinned potatoes

2 carrots, peeled

1 onion, peeled

2 summer squash

1 small zucchini

3 tablespoons oil

salt, to taste

pepper, to taste

optional additions: sweet potatoes, butternut squash, mushrooms, roasted garlic, red beets, parsnips

1 bunch fresh parsley, chopped, for garnish

1. Preheat the oven to 375°.
2. Scrub the potatoes and carrots well. Cut into 1-inch pieces.
3. Slice the onion crosswise so it's in wedges, not in rings.
4. Slice the summer squash and zucchini lengthwise, and then into 2-inch sticks.
5. Heat the oil in a 10-inch ovenproof skillet. Add the potatoes and carrots and sauté for several minutes.
6. Add the onion, summer squash, and zucchini. Sprinkle with salt and pepper.
7. Place the skillet in the oven and roast at 375° for 15 to 20 minutes or until the veggies are golden and test tender. (Some of the edges may begin to blacken.)
8. Remove from the oven, and add the chopped parsley.
9. Serve immediately.

# Pumpkin Soup

YVONNE MARTIN

*Serves 8 to 10*
*Prep Time: 10 minutes* ✇ *Cooking Time: 30 minutes*

¼ stick (2 tablespoons) butter

1 large onion, rough chopped

6 cups chicken broth, *divided*

2 cups cooked puréed pumpkin, *or* butternut squash

1 teaspoon salt

½ teaspoon pepper

1 teaspoon cinnamon

½ teaspoon ground ginger

1 cup half-and-half

3 tablespoons sour cream

1 tablespoon milk, *or* half-and-half

1. Melt the butter in a large pot. Add the onion and cook over medium heat for about 10 minutes until the onion is soft.
2. Add 3 cups of the chicken broth and simmer for about 20 minutes, or until it's reduced by half.
3. Add the remaining 3 cups of chicken broth. Using a hand blender, process the mixture in the pot until all the onion is puréed.
4. Mix in the cooked squash, salt, pepper, cinnamon, and ginger. Whisk together well.
5. Return to a simmer.
6. Immediately before serving, whisk in the half-and-half and heat through. But do not boil.
7. To garnish, combine 3 tablespoons of sour cream and 1 tablespoon of milk in a squeeze bottle. Shake well. Make concentric circles of the cream on the surface of the soup. If you wish, draw a knife or toothpick through the circles to give a webbed effect.

We do murder mysteries at the inn. Our actors LOVE this soup and request it every time they come here.

Guests are often skeptical about the idea of pumpkin soup,
but after one spoonful, they are asking for the recipe!

# Wake-Me-Up Salsa

DANIELLE HANSCOM

*Makes approximately 2¾ cups*
*Prep Time: 15 minutes*

1 cup diced tomatoes (diced small)*

1 cup diced green bell pepper (diced small)*

½ cup diced sweet onion (diced small)*

1 medium garlic clove, finely minced

1 fresh lime, juice only

2 tablespoons good extra-virgin olive oil

¼ teaspoon ground cumin

2 tablespoons chopped fresh cilantro

salt, freshly ground black pepper, and hot sauce,** to taste

1. Mix all the ingredients in a medium-size bowl. Cover with plastic wrap and refrigerate for at least an hour, but preferably overnight.
2. The salsa is also delicious on top of non-dairy polenta with slices of avocado as a vegan option, or in an omelet with thin slices of ripe avocado, or as a side to any eggs.

*\* I prefer to dice the tomatoes, peppers, and onion by hand. It looks much better on the plate.*

*\*\* I go easy on the hot sauce because I serve this salsa along with eggs for breakfast.*

A splash of color next to eggs on a plate is delightful. This salsa does just that, and it is absolutely delicious with eggs.

# Strawberry Salsa

KATHRYN WHITE

*Makes 3 to 4 cups*
*Prep Time: 10 to 12 minutes* 🌿 *Chilling Time: 60 minutes or more*

6 tablespoons olive oil

2 tablespoons white balsamic vinegar

½ teaspoon salt

1 pint fresh strawberries, coarsely chopped

4 green onions, chopped

2 pints cherry tomatoes, chopped

⅓ cup chopped fresh cilantro (use up to ½ cup if you like cilantro)

1. In a large bowl, whisk together the olive oil, vinegar, and salt.
2. Add the strawberries, onions, tomatoes, and cilantro, and toss.
3. Chill for at least an hour before serving.
4. Serve about ¼ cup on the side with eggs, or serve with corn chips.

When strawberries are in season, this is terrific served with chips, of course. But try it with eggs!

# Corn, Tomato, Beet, and Basil Salsa

ELLEN GUTMAN CHENAUX

*Serves 6*
*Prep Time: 10 minutes*

8 ears of corn, husked

3 tablespoons extra-virgin olive oil

½ cup chopped or thinly sliced fresh basil

5 tomatoes (plum tomatoes work best)

3 tablespoons balsamic vinegar

salt and pepper, to taste

½ cup red beets, cooked, peeled, and diced

1. Using a large knife, cut the raw corn kernels from the cobs into a good-sized bowl.
2. Add the olive oil, basil, tomatoes, and vinegar to the corn and mix together well.
3. Season to taste with salt and pepper.
4. You can serve the salsa immediately, or cover and chill it for up to 8 hours.
5. Add the beets just before serving to prevent them from turning the salsa red.

*So easy. So colorful. So delicious!*

# Gourmet Granola

JOYCE SCHULTE

*Makes about 1 gallon (36 ⅓-cup servings)*
*Prep Time: 55 minutes* ❧ *Baking Time: 30 minutes*

6 cups rolled oats

½ cup sesame seeds

¾ cup raw sunflower seeds

½ cup chopped pecans

1 cup chopped walnuts

1 cup dried coconut, unsweetened

½ cup raisins

½ cup dried cranberries

½ cup light vegetable oil

½ cup brown sugar, lightly packed

½ cup honey

½ cup maple syrup

¼ cup molasses

1 tablespoon vanilla extract

1½ teaspoons cinnamon

½ teaspoon salt

1. Preheat the oven to 350°. On 3 separate sheet pans (cookie sheets with rims work well), oven roast the oats for 20 to 30 minutes, the sesame and sunflower seeds for 10 to 15 minutes, and the pecans and walnuts for 8 to 10 minutes, until all are lightly toasted.
2. Remove the pans from the oven. (Do not turn off the oven.) Allow the ingredients to cool until just warm or at room temperature.
3. In a large bowl, combine all the toasted ingredients with the coconut, raisins, and dried cranberries. Set aside.
4. In a saucepan, combine the oil, brown sugar, honey, maple syrup, molasses, vanilla, cinnamon. Stir over low heat until well combined and warm to the touch. But do NOT boil!
5. Pour the liquid mixture over the dry mixture and mix well.
6. Grease 2 sheet pans. Divide the mixture between the pans so that the ingredients have as much contact with the bottom of the pan as possible.

7. Roast at 350° for about 30 minutes, stirring every 10 minutes, or just until the granola is browned to your liking.
8. Remove from the oven and cool. Then store in tightly-sealed containers in a cool, dry place.

---

Granola has been a must-have for breakfast at our inn. We had a challenge, however, because granolas have nuts, and I have a terrible nut allergy. But I am able to eat pecans and walnuts. After reading an untold number of recipes that wouldn't work, my husband created his own recipe. We served this granola every day for 19 years!

# Sauces, Toppings, and Condiments

## Oh, My!

# Versatile Simple Syrups

DANIELLE HANSCOM

*Makes 1½ cups*
*Prep Time: 3 to 10 minutes ❧ Cooking Time: 2 to 5 minutes*

1 cup granulated sugar

1 cup water

**Note:** *Simple syrups can be kept in the refrigerator for up to 2 weeks.*

1. Mix both ingredients in a small saucepan and bring to a quick boil over high heat.
2. Remove from the heat immediately. Stir to make sure the sugar is completely dissolved.
3. While the sugar water is still hot, add one of the following and steep until cool:
   - The zest of 2 well-scrubbed lemons
   - The zest of 2 well-scrubbed oranges
   - 1 inch of grated, fresh, peeled gingerroot
   - A handful of chopped mint leaves
   - A combination of herbs of your choice
4. When the syrup is cold, strain it into a jar fitted with an airtight screw top. Discard the solids.

A tablespoon or two of a flavored simple syrup can really add a bit of zing to any fruit dish. We use the mint syrup on a pineapple and kiwi fruit cup and garnish it with a mint leaf. A tablespoon or two of lemon syrup added to sliced strawberries is wonderful served over Matthew's Biscuits (page 60). The ginger syrup is amazing on a tropical fruit salad with mango, pineapple, star fruit, and papaya.

# Bourbon Pecan Syrup

ELLEN GUTMAN CHENAUX

*Serves 12*

*Prep Time: 5 minutes*  *Cooking Time: 3 to 5 minutes*

1 cup maple syrup

¼ to ⅓ cup bourbon

¾ cup pecans, lightly toasted

1. In a small saucepan, mix the maple syrup and bourbon together.
2. Cook over medium heat until the syrup begins to bubble.
3. Add the pecans just before serving.
4. Pour over French toast, pancakes, or ice cream.

Add a touch of "southern comfort" to pancakes, waffles, French toast, and, yes, even ice cream!

# Caramel Sauce

KATHRYN WHITE

*Makes 4 cups*
*Prep Time: 5 minutes* 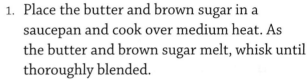 *Cooking Time: 5 minutes*

2 sticks (½ pound) butter

2¼ cups brown sugar, lightly packed

1 pint heavy cream

1 teaspoon vanilla

1. Place the butter and brown sugar in a saucepan and cook over medium heat. As the butter and brown sugar melt, whisk until thoroughly blended.
2. Remove from the heat and add the heavy cream slowly so it doesn't bubble over. Blend with the whisk, and then add the vanilla. Stir. Be careful! The caramel is very hot!

**Notes:** *Dip apple slices into the sauce. And it can even be stirred into your morning coffee or latte.*

*The sauce can be stored in a glass jar and refrigerated for a week. To reheat, place the sauce in a saucepan over low heat until warmed. Stir frequently so it doesn't stick.*

Over ice cream. Over French toast. Over pound cake. Need I say more?

# Vanilla Sauce

DEBBIE MOSIMANN

*Makes 1½ cups*
*Prep Time: 15 minutes  ❧  Cooking Time: 3 to 5 minutes*

1 cup water

⅔ cup sugar

1 tablespoon cornstarch

pinch of salt

¼ stick (2 tablespoons) butter, cut into chunks

2 teaspoons vanilla

1. Bring the water to a boil in a saucepan.
2. In a small bowl, combine the sugar, cornstarch, and salt.
3. Whisk the sugar/cornstarch mixture into the hot water. Bring to a full boil, stirring constantly until thickened.
4. Remove from the heat.
5. Add the butter and whisk until melted and incorporated.
6. Stir in the vanilla.
7. Serve warm over bread pudding or plum pudding.

My childhood Christmas dinners always included a steamed plum pudding topped with this vanilla sauce. It was the crowning glory we all looked forward to every year.

As an adult, it dawned on me that I didn't have to wait until Christmas to make and serve the sauce. Surely there was something else I could ladle it over at another time of the year. Today I top the likes of sticky bun bread pudding and bourbon pumpkin bread pudding with this Vanilla Sauce, much to everyone's delight!

Such a Plain Jane name for such an amazingly flavorful and versatile sauce!

# Arkansas Chocolate Gravy

KRISTIE ROSSET

*Serves 6*
*Prep Time: 10 minutes* ✕ *Cooking Time: 15 minutes*

1 stick (8 tablespoons) butter

4 tablespoons cocoa powder

4 tablespoons flour

¾ cup sugar

2 cups milk

1. Melt the butter in a small saucepan.
2. Add the cocoa and flour, whisking until well combined.
3. Stir in the sugar and milk.
4. Cook over medium heat until thickened, whisking constantly.
5. Serve over biscuits and enjoy every bite.

**Note:** *We love to serve this atop Matthew's Biscuits (page 60).*

This surprisingly tasty breakfast treat is an old Southern country recipe from my son-in-law's family. What an extraordinary way for chocolate lovers to begin their day!

# Blueberry Sauce

ELLEN GUTMAN CHENAUX

*Serves 12*
*Prep Time: 1 minute* ❧ *Cooking Time: 3 to 5 minutes*

2 cups blueberries, fresh *or* frozen (preferably, the small wild blueberries)

½ cup sugar

juice of half a lemon, freshly squeezed

1 tablespoon cornstarch

1½ tablespoons orange juice

1. Combine the blueberries, sugar, and lemon juice in a medium-size saucepan.
2. Stirring frequently, cook over medium heat until the sugar is dissolved and the mixture begins to bubble.
3. In a small bowl, mix the cornstarch and orange juice together until smooth. Add this mixture to the blueberries and stir.
4. Continue cooking, stirring frequently, until the sauce is thickened.

*Lemon gives blueberries a great tang. Add this sauce to just about anything and away you go!*

# Lemon Sauce

KATHRYN WHITE AND LYNNETTE SCOFIELD

*Makes about 2½ cups*
*Prep Time: 5 to 7 minutes    Cooking Time: 3 to 8 minutes*

1 cup sugar

2 to 3 tablespoons cornstarch

2 cups water

half a stick (4 tablespoons)
butter, cut into chunks

2 to 3 tablespoons
grated lemon peel

¼ cup lemon juice

1. In a small pan, mix the sugar with the cornstarch.
2. Stir in the water until smooth. Bring the mixture to a boil over high heat, stirring frequently.
3. Remove from the heat. Stir in the butter, grated lemon peel, and lemon juice. Continue stirring until the butter melts. Serve warm.

This Lemon Sauce pairs well with a variety of dishes: blueberry pancakes, pound cake and yellow cakes, as a topping for tropical fruit, and accompanying a fruit platter. We love the zing of lemon!

# Lemon Curd

YVONNE MARTIN

*Makes 2 cups*
*Prep time: 15 minutes  Cooking time: 5 minutes*

3 eggs, beaten

1 cup sugar

½ cup fresh lemon juice

1 tablespoon grated lemon rind

half a stick (¼ cup) butter,
cut into chunks

1. In a medium-sized heavy saucepan, combine all of the ingredients.
2. Cook over low heat, stirring constantly until thickened, for about 5 minutes on simmer.
3. Let cool. Store in a covered jar in the refrigerator.

**Note:** *Use the curd within 2 weeks.*

While lemon curd is the traditional accompaniment to tea scones, it also makes a great filling for stuffed French toast or a mini tart. And it tastes great folded into whipped cream and then spooned over fresh berries for a light summer dessert.

# Crème Fraîche

KRISTIE ROSSET

*Makes 1¼ cups*
*Prep Time: 5 minutes*

1 cup sour cream

⅛ cup heavy cream

⅛ cup brown sugar

½ teaspoon vanilla

1. Mix all ingredients together gently in a medium-sized bowl.
2. Dollop onto a dessert just before serving for a delicious finishing touch.

**Note:** *This will keep for up to 2 weeks, covered, in the refrigerator.*

Top almost anything on the sweet side with crème fraîche:
a bowl of berries, grilled watermelon (page 26), pound cake,
or bread pudding. Plus the fancy name makes it sound
like you really know what you're doing in the kitchen!

# Cilantro Butter

LYNNETTE SCOFIELD

*Makes ¼ cup*
*Prep Time: 10 minutes* ✺ *Chilling Time: an hour or more*

1 stick (8 tablespoons)
unsalted butter, softened
to room temperature

1 teaspoon salt

2 tablespoons fresh
cilantro leaves, chopped

1. Mix the butter, salt, and cilantro with a hand mixer on a low speed.
2. Spoon onto a piece of plastic wrap and form into a log.
3. Refrigerate for an hour or more.
4. When ready to serve, slice into rounds.

**Note:** *This can be prepared ahead and frozen for later use.*

*Takes minutes to make and rewards you with a tremendous amount of flavor!*

# Mustard

DEBBIE MOSIMANN

*Makes ¾ cup*
*Prep Time: 10 minutes* ❧ *Cooking Time: 10 minutes*

1 tablespoon whole mustard seeds

⅓ cup water

½ cup dry mustard

⅓ cup cider vinegar

1½ teaspoons turmeric

1 clove garlic, minced

1 tablespoon honey

1 teaspoon salt

1 egg yolk

1. Measure the mustard seeds and water into a small bowl. Set them aside.
2. Measure the dry mustard, vinegar, turmeric, garlic, honey, and salt into a small saucepan.
3. Add the mustard seeds and water.
4. Bring the mixture to a boil. Boil for 3 minutes, stirring constantly
5. Remove from the heat. Quickly whisk in the egg yolk.
6. Set aside to cool.

**Note:** *To make a cream cheese mustard spread, soften 8 ounces of cream cheese to room temperature in a mixing bowl. Beat it until soft. Then beat in 3 tablespoons of mustard. Refrigerate till needed. Bring the mixture to room temperature before serving.*

Small dollops of mustard pair well with breakfast meats, as a side to cheese on the afternoon tray, and mixed with cream cheese for a spicy dip. Making your own is far easier than you might think!

We also love to dip soft pretzels into this homemade hot mustard mixed with cream cheese. Be forewarned, it has some kick!

# Hot Water Hollandaise

### DEBBIE MOSIMANN

*Makes 1¼ cups or 10 servings*
*Prep Time: 5 minutes* ✺ *Cooking Time: 10 minutes*

water for a
double boiler

2 egg yolks

1 tablespoon
hot water

1 tablespoon
lemon juice

pinch of salt

2 sticks (1 cup)
cold, unsalted
butter, cut
into pieces

pepper, to taste

1. In the bottom part of a double boiler, bring the water to a slow simmer.
2. Whisk the egg yolks, 1 tablespoon of hot water, the lemon juice, and salt together in the top part of the double boiler. Put the top part over the simmering water (the top part should not touch the simmering water below) and whisk.
3. As the egg yolks warm, add 1 or 2 pieces of the cold butter and whisk until the butter is almost melted. Then add another 2 pieces of butter, continuing to do so until all the butter is melted into the eggs and the whole mixture is creamy and opaque.
4. With a spoon, taste to make sure the flavor is where you want it. Add salt and pepper to taste. If you need more lemon, you can add a bit of lemon zest. The sauce will be the consistency of heavy cream.
5. Remove from the top of the double boiler and serve over Eggs Benedict or salmon filets.

**Note:** *Leftovers will hold in a covered container in the refrigerator for several days. It will solidify into what feels like a soft butter. To serve, gently warm over hot water and serve.*

While searching for the perfect no-fail Hollandaise recipe to teach to others, I came across this method, and I've never looked back. It is so easy, the result so silky smooth, creamy, and not runny—it's all but foolproof.

Serve over poached salmon, or allow it to cool and then fold into deviled egg filling. You may find yourself licking the spoon.

# Drinks

## Chilled and Heated

You can incorporate any frozen fruit. This is a great way to use over-ripe bananas. Just slice bananas into bite-size pieces and freeze them in packets, each holding half a banana. Using frozen bananas and other frozen fruit eliminates the need for ice or sweeteners. For this photo I made a peach smoothie and a mixed berry smoothie.

# Berry Smoothie

KRISTIE ROSSET

*Makes 1 smoothie*
*Prep Time: 10 minutes*

½ banana, frozen *or* fresh

1 cup frozen fruit of your choice (use organic if you can)

1 tablespoon PB Fit (peanut butter powder)

2 teaspoons organic chia seeds

1 cup unsweetened vanilla almond milk (or other milk of your choosing)

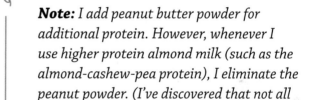

1. Put all the ingredients in a blender. Set blender to "smoothie" setting, and blend away. It may take a couple of stirs and spins at this setting.
2. Pour into a glass and enjoy a healthy and refreshing breakfast.

**Note:** *I add peanut butter powder for additional protein. However, whenever I use higher protein almond milk (such as the almond-cashew-pea protein), I eliminate the peanut powder. (I've discovered that not all stores carry the high protein milk.)*

Like many of you, I am using less meat in my diet and increasing plant-based foods. This fruit smoothie is satisfying for breakfast and sustains me for hours. For a more complete breakfast, I eat a handful of nuts after enjoying the smoothie.

# Some Like It... Cold!
# Cold-Brewed Iced Coffee

ELLEN CHENAUX

*Prep Time: 5 minutes*
*Chilling Time: 12 to 24 hours*

Making cold-brewed iced coffee involves steeping the ground coffee in cold water for 12 to 24 hours. It's the process that sells the coffee.

Cold-brewed iced coffee is richer because of the bean-to-water ratio, and because of the lengthy steeping/brewing time. Time, as opposed to heat, extracts more of the coffee's oils, sugar, and, of course, caffeine.

*Cold-brewing creates a really smooth buzz!*

1. First you need a large container, French press, or Mason jar, deep enough to hold the coffee and water.
2. Ratio: ¼ pound fresh, coarsely ground lighter roast beans to 4 cups of room-temperature water. (You can easily double, triple, or go higher with these amounts. Just maintain the proportions.)
3. Place the coffee grounds in your container. If you are using a French press, pour the coffee into the bottom of the canister.
4. Gradually add the water, allowing the water to slowly dampen the ground coffee as you pour.
5. Gently stir to just moisten all of the coffee.
6. Cover and let stand for at least 12 hours.
7. Line a fine mesh sieve with cheesecloth or even pantyhose. Pour the coffee through the sieve, making sure that all the coffee has filtered out. If you are using a French press, press the plunger down to separate the grounds from the water. Pour.
8. This concentrate—covered and chilled—keeps for up to two weeks.
9. When ready to serve, dilute—I suggest a 1:1 ratio—with ice, milk, or whatever you like.
10. And enjoy the buzz!

# Hot Apple Cider

ELLEN GUTMAN CHENAUX

*Serves 6*
*Prep Time: 5 to 30 minutes*

**For Basic Hot Cider:**

6 cups apple cider

1 cinnamon stick

When it's chilly outside, it's time for some hot comfort inside – a roaring fire and a cup of hot cider. The secret to great hot cider is the cider itself, preferably from your local apple orchard or farmers market. There are so many variations of hot cider – be creative!

1. Heat the cider and cinnamon stick in a large saucepan over medium high heat for 5 to 10 minutes. Serve piping hot.

### Variations:

*Add any or all of these ingredients to 6 cups apple cider. Heat to steamy for 5 to 10 minutes. Then simmer for another 15 minutes.*

¼ cup real maple syrup

juice of ½ lemon

3 whole cloves

3 allspice berries

peel of one orange, cut into strips

peel of one lemon, cut into strips

3 tablespoons butter

½ cup rum, *or* 1 cup red wine

# French Hot Chocolate

DEBBIE MOSIMANN

*Serves 8 to 10*
*Prep Time: 10 minutes* ❧ *Chilling Time: 30 to 55 minutes*

1 cup whipping cream

1 cup good quality dark chocolate, 61% cacao or higher

1 tablespoon unsweetened cocoa powder

1 tablespoon water

4 cups milk

1. In a non-reactive pan heat the whipping cream to just under boiling. Measure the chocolate into a bowl. Pour the cream over the chocolate and stir to melt. This is a traditional ganache.
2. Combine the cocoa powder and water in a small bowl. Then stir it into the chocolate mixture.
3. Allow that mixture to cool for 10 minutes. Then place it in the refrigerator for 20 to 45 minutes, or until the mix is set but not hardened.
4. With the whisk attachment of your mixer, whip for 4 to 5 minutes, until it reaches a smooth, frosting-like consistency.
5. Spoon about 3 tablespoons of the mixture into heat-proof glasses or small mugs.
6. Pour hot milk over top. Stir gently. Then serve

*Rich and creamy is the outcome of this recipe for hot chocolate that is second to none. Use the best cocoa powder you can find for best results. A teaspoon of Grand Marnier or a sprinkle of crushed peppermint candy adds a twist of flavor.*

# Recipe Index

## A

**Almonds**
Baked Apricots, 14
**Apple Cider**
Hot Apple Cider, 233
Apple Sausage Bake, 188
**Apples**
Apple Sausage Bake, 188
Baked Apples, 10
Ham, Apple, and Goat Cheese Breakfast Toast, 189
Lemon Brandied Apples, 11
Omelet with Variations, 124
Outrageously Great Waffles—with Flavor Options, 106
Scandinavian Apple Pancake, 120
Sweet Potato Hash, 190
Applesauce Date Muffins, 44
**Applesauce**
Applesauce Date Muffins, 44
Apricot Walnut Muffins, 45
**Apricots**
Apricot Walnut Muffins, 45
Baked Apricots, 14
Arkansas Chocolate Gravy, 217
**Artichokes**
Crab and Artichoke Egg Puff, 153
Veggie Frittata, 133

**Arugula**
Smoked Salmon Avocado Toast, 166
Asparagus Goat Cheese Crustless Quiche, 139
**Asparagus**
Asparagus Goat Cheese Crustless Quiche, 139
Garden Baked Eggs, 150
Veggie Frittata, 133
**Avocados**
Grilled Cheese Bacon-Avocado-Tomato Sandwich (aka "Cheese & BAT"), 165
Smoked Salmon Avocado Toast, 166

## B

**Bacon**
Glazed Bacon, 186
Grilled Cheese Bacon-Avocado-Tomato Sandwich (aka "Cheese & BAT"), 165
Omelet with Variations, 124
Baked Apples, 10
Baked Apricots, 14
Baked Oatmeal, 112
Banana Sour Cream Pancakes, 84
**Bananas**
Banana Sour Cream Pancakes, 84
Berry Smoothie, 231
Blueberry/Blackberry Yogurt Parfait, 38
Outrageously Great Waffles—with Flavor Options, 106

Basil and Tomato Egg Scramble, 159

**Basil, Fresh**

Basil and Tomato Egg Scramble, 159

Corn, Tomato, Beet, and Basil Salsa, 207

Kiss My Grits!, 180

Parmesan Heirloom Cherry Tomatoes, 198

Tomato Basil Pie, 136

Tri-Color Terrine, 130

**Beans, Black**

Black Bean and Tortilla Strata, 170

Breakfast Burrito, 172

**Beets, Red**

Corn, Tomato, Beet, and Basil Salsa, 207

Berry Smoothie, 231

Birchermuesli, 40

**Biscuits**

Matthew's Buttermilk Biscuits, 60

Black Bean and Tortilla Strata, 170

**Blackberries**

Baked Oatmeal, 112

Blueberry/Blackberry Yogurt Parfait, 38

**Blintz**

Orange Blintz Bake, 114

**Blueberries**

Baked Oatmeal, 112

Blueberry/Blackberry Yogurt Parfait, 38

Blueberry Bread Pudding with Orange
Custard, 118

Blueberry Buttermilk Muffins with Streusel
Topping, 46

Blueberry Coffee Cake, 62

Blueberry Cornmeal Pancakes, 87

Blueberry Pecan Waffles, 110

Blueberry Sauce, 218

Blueberry Sour Cream Pancakes with Lemon
Sauce, 88

Orange Blintz Bake, 114

Outrageously Great Waffles—with Flavor
Options, 106

Blueberry/Blackberry Yogurt Parfait, 38

Blueberry Bread Pudding with Orange Custard,
118

Blueberry Buttermilk Muffins with Streusel
Topping, 46

Blueberry Coffee Cake, 62

Blueberry Cornmeal Pancakes, 87

Blueberry Pecan Waffles, 110

Blueberry Sauce, 218

Blueberry Sour Cream Pancakes with Lemon
Sauce, 88

Bourbon Pecan Syrup, 214

**Bourbon**

Bourbon Pecan Syrup, 214

**Brandy**

Lemon Brandied Apples, 11

Mushroom Crepes with Shiitake & Spinach
Sauce, 174

**Bread**

Apple Sausage Bake, 188

Blueberry Bread Pudding with Orange
Custard, 118

Caramel Peach Bread Pudding, 116

Cranberry French Toast, 102

Cranberry-Orange Bread, 66

Decadent Chocolate French Toast with
Strawberry Syrup, 104

Fondue Florentine Soufflé, 148

Grilled Cheese Bacon-Avocado-Tomato
Sandwich (aka "Cheese & BAT"), 165

Ham, Apple, and Goat Cheese Breakfast Toast, 189

Honey Oat Bread, 74

Huevos Trifecta, 156

Melodious Poppy Seed Bread, 72

Mushroom Sausage Bread Pudding, 178

Peach-Nectarine Upside-Down French Toast, 100

Pear Pecan Cardamom Bread, 69

Pumpkin Bread, 70

Shakshouka Flatbread, 176

Smoked Salmon Avocado Toast, 166

Smoked Salmon Eggs Benedict, 163

Sunflower Pumpkin Bread, 71

Tomatoes Benedict, 160

Breakfast Burrito, 172

**Broccoli**

Garden Baked Eggs, 150

**Buns**

Cinnamon Buns, 76

**Burritos**

Breakfast Burrito, 172

**Butter**

Cilantro Butter, 223

**Buttermilk**

Blueberry Buttermilk Muffins with Streusel Topping, 46

Blueberry Coffee Cake, 62

Blueberry Pecan Waffles, 110

Chocolate Chip Buttermilk Pancakes, 98

Matthew's Buttermilk Biscuits, 60

Outrageously Great Waffles—with Flavor Options, 106

Ray's Strawberry Soup, 37

Spice Pancakes with Lemon Sauce, 94

Strawberry Rhubarb Coffee Cake, 64

Whole Wheat Pancakes with Roasted Pecans, 96

**Butternut Squash** *See Squash, Butternut*

## C

**Cantaloupe**

Grilled Watermelon Topped with Mango Salsa and Crème Fraîche, 26

Caramelized Onion Omelet, 126

Caramel Peach Bread Pudding, 116

Caramel Sauce, 215

**Carrots**

Roasted Fall Root Vegetables, 201

**Challah**

Decadent Chocolate French Toast with Strawberry Syrup, 104

Peach-Nectarine Upside-Down French Toast, 100

**Cheese, Asiago**

Tomatoes Benedict, 160

**Cheese, Cheddar**

Breakfast Burrito, 172

Creamy Polenta or Grits, 196

Garden Baked Eggs, 150

Grilled Cheese Bacon-Avocado-Tomato Sandwich (aka "Cheese & BAT"), 165

Ham and Cheese Rolled Omelet, 129

Ham Baked Eggs, 154

Kiss My Grits!, 180

Mediterranean Quiche, 140

Northwest Salmon Breakfast Pie, 145

Omelet with Variations, 124

Southwest Sausage Strata, 168

Spinach and Leek Soufflé, 146

Spinach Brownies, 183

Summer Frittata, 134

Tomatoes Benedict, 160

Tri-Color Terrine, 130

Veggie Frittata, 133

**Cheese, Colby**

Grilled Cheese Bacon-Avocado-Tomato
Sandwich (aka "Cheese & BAT"), 165

**Cheese, Cottage**

Crab and Artichoke Egg Puff, 153

Mediterranean Quiche, 140

Orange Blintz Bake, 114

Spinach and Leek Soufflé, 146

**Cheese, Cream**

Blueberry Bread Pudding with Orange
Custard, 118

Breakfast Burrito, 172

Cinnamon Buns, 76

Cranberry French Toast, 102

Ham and Cheese Rolled Omelet, 129

Orange Blintz Bake, 114

Pineapple Napoleon, 22

Spinach and Leek Soufflé, 146

**Cheese, Emmentaler**

Mushroom Sausage Bread Pudding, 178

**Cheese, Feta**

Basil and Tomato Egg Scramble, 159

Mediterranean Quiche, 140

Summer Frittata, 134

**Cheese, Fontina**

Maryland Blue Crab Quiche, 142

**Cheese, Goat**

Asparagus Goat Cheese Crustless Quiche, 139

Ham, Apple, and Goat Cheese Breakfast Toast,
189

**Cheese, Gouda**

Caramelized Onion Omelet, 126

**Cheese, Gruyère**

Fondue Florentine Soufflé, 148

Mushroom Sausage Bread Pudding, 178

Omelet with Variations, 124

**Cheese, Monterey Jack**

Black Bean and Tortilla Strata, 170

Breakfast Burrito, 172

Crab and Artichoke Egg Puff, 153

Maryland Blue Crab Quiche, 142

Veggie Frittata, 133

**Cheese, Parmesan**

Ham Baked Eggs, 154

Kiss My Grits!, 180

Parmesan Heirloom Cherry Tomatoes, 198

Tomato Basil Pie, 136

Tomatoes Benedict, 160

Veggie Frittata, 133

**Cheese, Pepper Jack**

Breakfast Burrito, 172

Grilled Cheese Bacon-Avocado-Tomato
Sandwich (aka "Cheese & BAT"), 165

**Cheese, Provolone**

Grilled Cheese Bacon-Avocado-Tomato
Sandwich (aka "Cheese & BAT"), 165

**Cheese, Ricotta**

Lemon Ricotta Pancake, 85

Orange Blintz Bake, 114

Tomato Basil Pie, 136

**Cheese, Swiss**
Ham Baked Eggs, 154

**Cherries, Sour**
Upside-Down Sour Cherry Muffins, 48

**Chilies, Green**
Breakfast Burrito, 172

**Chilies, Green Canned**
Southwest Sausage Strata, 168

Chilled Peach Soup, 34

**Chives**
Basil and Tomato Egg Scramble, 159
Garden Baked Eggs, 150
Parmesan Heirloom Cherry Tomatoes, 198

**Chocolate**
Arkansas Chocolate Gravy, 217
French Hot Chocolate, 234

Chocolate Chip Buttermilk Pancakes, 98

**Chocolate Chips**
Chocolate Chip Buttermilk Pancakes, 98

**Chocolate Chips, White**
White Chocolate and Cranberry Tea Scones, 57

**Cider**
Hot Apple Cider, 233

Cilantro Butter, 223

**Cilantro, Fresh**
Cilantro Butter, 223
Strawberry Salsa, 205
Wake-Me-Up Salsa, 204

Cinnamon Buns, 76

Cinnamon Syrup, 93

**Coconut, Dried**
Gourmet Granola, 208

**Coffee**
Some Like It... Cold! Cold-Brewed Iced Coffee, 232

**Coffee Cake**
Blueberry Coffee Cake, 62
Strawberry Rhubarb Coffee Cake, 64

**Compote**
Spiced Peach Compote, 32

Corn, Tomato, Beet, and Basil Salsa, 207

**Corn**
Corn, Tomato, Beet, and Basil Salsa, 207
Mini Corn Cakes, 182

**Cornmeal**
Blueberry Cornmeal Pancakes, 87
Strawberry Cornmeal Muffins, 53

**Cottage Cheese** *See Cheese, Cottage*

Crab and Artichoke Egg Puff, 153

**Crabmeat**
Crab and Artichoke Egg Puff, 153
Maryland Blue Crab Quiche, 142

**Cranberries, Dried**
Gourmet Granola, 208
Sunflower Pumpkin Bread, 71
White Chocolate and Cranberry Tea Scones, 57

**Cranberries, Fresh**
Cranberry French Toast, 102
Cranberry-Orange Bread, 66

Cranberry French Toast, 102

Cranberry-Orange Bread, 66

Cranberry-Raspberry Poached Pears, 18

**Cranberry Juice**
Cranberry-Raspberry Poached Pears, 18

**Cream Cheese** *See Cheese, Cream*

**Cream of Wheat**
Griess Schnitten (Cream of Wheat Squares), 113
Creamy Polenta or Grits, 196
Crème Fraîche, 222
**Crepes**
Mushroom Crepes with Shiitake & Spinach Sauce, 174
**Curd**
Lemon Curd, 220
**Custard**
Blueberry Bread Pudding with Orange Custard, 118
Orange Custard, 119

**Dates**
Applesauce Date Muffins, 44
Decadent Chocolate French Toast with Strawberry Syrup, 104

**Eggs**
Asparagus Goat Cheese Crustless Quiche, 139
Basil and Tomato Egg Scramble, 159
Black Bean and Tortilla Strata, 170
Blueberry Bread Pudding with Orange Custard, 118

Breakfast Burrito, 172
Caramelized Onion Omelet, 126
Caramel Peach Bread Pudding, 116
Crab and Artichoke Egg Puff, 153
Cranberry French Toast, 102
Decadent Chocolate French Toast with Strawberry Syrup, 104
Fondue Florentine Soufflé, 148
Garden Baked Eggs, 150
Ham and Cheese Rolled Omelet, 129
Ham Baked Eggs, 154
Huevos Trifecta, 156
Lemon Curd, 220
Maryland Blue Crab Quiche, 142
Mediterranean Quiche, 140
Mushroom Sausage Bread Pudding, 178
Omelet with Variations, 124
Orange Custard, 119
Peach-Nectarine Upside-Down French Toast, 100
Shakshouka Flatbread, 176
Smoked Salmon Eggs Benedict, 163
Southwest Sausage Strata, 168
Summer Frittata, 134
Tomatoes Benedict, 160
Tri-Color Terrine, 130
Veggie Frittata, 133
**Eggs, Scrambled**
Basil and Tomato Egg Scramble, 159
English Muffins, 80
**English Muffins**
Huevos Trifecta, 156
Tomatoes Benedict, 160

Fig and Kumquat Scones, 59
**Figs**
  Fig and Kumquat Scones, 59
Fondue Florentine Soufflé, 148
French Hot Chocolate, 234
**French Toast**
  Cranberry French Toast, 102
  Decadent Chocolate French Toast with
    Strawberry Syrup, 104
  Peach-Nectarine Upside-Down French Toast, 100
**Frittata**
  Summer Frittata, 134
  Veggie Frittata, 133

G

Garden Baked Eggs, 150
Ginger Spice Pancakes, 92
**Ginger**
  Ginger Spice Pancakes, 92
  Pomegranate Ginger Muffins, 50
  Pumpkin-Ginger Pancakes, 90
  Versatile Simple Syrups, 212
**Ginger, Candied**
  Lemon Ginger Rolls, 78
Glazed Bacon, 186
Gourmet Granola, 208
**Grand Marnier**
  Blueberry Bread Pudding with Orange
    Custard, 118

Decadent Chocolate French Toast with
  Strawberry Syrup, 104
Granola Pancakes, 95
**Granola**
  Blueberry/Blackberry Yogurt Parfait, 38
  Gourmet Granola, 208
  Granola Pancakes, 95
  Oatmeal Granola Muffins, 55
**Grapefruit**
  Pomegranate Pear Salad, or Winter Fruit
    Salad, 13
  Sunny Morning Citrus, 15
**Grapes, Red**
  Birchermuesli, 40
**Green Chilies**
  Breakfast Burrito, 172
**Green Chilies, Canned**
  Southwest Sausage Strata, 168
**Green Onions**
  Ham and Cheese Rolled Omelet, 129
Griess Schnitten (Cream of Wheat Squares), 113
Grilled Cheese Bacon-Avocado-Tomato
  Sandwich (aka "Cheese & BAT"), 165
Grilled Peaches or Nectarines, 31
Grilled Watermelon Topped with Mango Salsa
  and Crème Fraîche, 26
**Grilling**
  Grilled Peaches or Nectarines, 31
  Grilled Watermelon Topped with Mango Salsa
    and Crème Fraîche, 26
**Grits**
  Creamy Polenta or Grits, 196
  Kiss My Grits!, 180

# H

Ham and Cheese Rolled Omelet, 129
Ham, Apple, and Goat Cheese Breakfast Toast, 189
Ham Baked Eggs, 154
**Ham**
    Ham and Cheese Rolled Omelet, 129
    Ham, Apple, and Goat Cheese Breakfast Toast, 189
    Ham Baked Eggs, 154
**Hash**
    Sweet Potato Hash, 190
**Hollandaise Sauce**
    Hot Water Hollandaise, 226
    Smoked Salmon Eggs Benedict, 163
Honey Oat Bread, 74
Hot Apple Cider, 233
**Hot Chocolate**
    French Hot Chocolate, 234
Hot Water Hollandaise, 226
Huevos Trifecta, 156

# I

**Ice Cream**
    Pineapple Sunrise, 25

# K

**Kale**
    Tri-Color Terrine, 130

Kiss My Grits!, 180
**Kumquats**
    Fig and Kumquat Scones, 59

# L

**Leeks**
    Potato Veggie Pancakes, 167
    Spinach and Leek Soufflé, 146
Lemon Brandied Apples, 11
Lemon Curd, 220
Lemon Ginger Rolls, 78
Lemon Ricotta Pancakes, 85
Lemon Sauce, 89
Lemon Sauce, 219
**Lemons**
    Blueberry Sour Cream Pancakes with Lemon Sauce, 88
    Decadent Chocolate French Toast with Strawberry Syrup, 104
    Lemon Curd, 220
    Lemon Ginger Rolls, 78
    Lemon Ricotta Pancake, 85
    Lemon Sauce, 89
    Lemon Sauce, 219
    Outrageously Great Waffles—with Flavor Options, 106
    Versatile Simple Syrups, 212
**Limes**
    Mango Tango, 21

# M

Mango Tango, 21

**Mangoes**

Grilled Watermelon Topped with Mango Salsa
and Crème Fraîche, 26

Mango Tango, 21

**Maple Syrup**

Stewed Plums, 29

**Marmalade**

Cranberry French Toast, 102

Orange Blintz Bake, 114

Maryland Blue Crab Quiche, 142

Matthew's Buttermilk Biscuits, 60

Mediterr'anean Quiche, 140

Meet the Eight Broads in the Kitchen!, 253

Melodious Poppy Seed Bread, 72

Mini Corn Cakes, 182

**Mint, Fresh**

Versatile Simple Syrups, 212

**Molasses**

Shoofly Pie Muffins, 56

**Muffins**

Applesauce Date Muffins, 44

Apricot Walnut Muffins, 45

Blueberry Buttermilk Muffins with Streusel
Topping, 46

English Muffins, 80

Oat Bran Muffin Mix, 54

Oatmeal Granola Muffins, 55

Pomegranate Ginger Muffins, 50

Shoofly Pie Muffins, 56

Strawberry Cornmeal Muffins, 53

Upside-Down Sour Cherry Muffins, 48

Mushroom Crepes with Shiitake & Spinach
Sauce, 174

Mushroom Sausage Bread Pudding, 178

**Mushrooms**

Garden Baked Eggs, 150

Mushroom Sausage Bread Pudding, 178

Omelet with Variations, 124

Potato Veggie Pancakes, 167

**Mushrooms, Shiitake**

Mushroom Crepes with Shiitake & Spinach
Sauce, 174

Mustard, 224

**Mustard Seeds**

Mustard, 224

*Blueberry Buttermilk Muffins with Streusel Topping, 46*

# N

Neapolitan Potatoes, 192

**Nectarines**

Grilled Peaches or Nectarines, 31

Peach-Nectarine Upside-Down French Toast, 100

Northwest Salmon Breakfast Pie, 145

# O

Oat Bran Muffin Mix, 54

**Oat Bran**

Oat Bran Muffin Mix, 54

Oatmeal Granola Muffins, 55

**Oatmeal**

Baked Oatmeal, 112

**Oats, Dry**

Oat Bran Muffin Mix, 54

**Oats, Quick**

Apricot Walnut Muffins, 45

Baked Oatmeal, 112

Honey Oat Bread, 74

Oatmeal Granola Muffins, 55

Spice Pancakes with Lemon Sauce, 94

**Oats, Rolled**

Baked Oatmeal, 112

Birchermuesli, 40

Gourmet Granola, 208

Granola Pancakes, 95

Omelet with Variations, 124

**Omelet**

Caramelized Onion Omelet, 126

Ham and Cheese Rolled Omelet, 129

Omelet with Variations, 124

**Onion, Green**

Ham and Cheese Rolled Omelet, 129

Strawberry Salsa, 205

**Onions**

Caramelized Onion Omelet, 126

Northwest Salmon Breakfast Pie, 145

Roasted Fall Root Vegetables, 201

Summer Frittata, 134

Orange Blintz Bake, 114

Orange Custard, 119

**Orange Liqueur**

Poached Pears with Orange Glaze, 16

**Oranges**

Orange Custard, 119

Outrageously Great Waffles—with Flavor Options, 106

Poached Pears with Orange Glaze, 16

Sunny Morning Citrus, 15

Versatile Simple Syrups, 212

**Oranges, Mandarin**

Birchermuesli, 40

Outrageously Great Waffles—with Flavor Options, 106

# P

**Pancakes**
Banana Sour Cream Pancakes, 84
Blueberry Cornmeal Pancakes, 87
Blueberry Sour Cream Pancakes with Lemon
 Sauce, 88
Chocolate Chip Buttermilk Pancakes, 98
Ginger Spice Pancakes, 92
Granola Pancakes, 95
Lemon Ricotta Pancake, 85
Potato Veggie Pancakes, 167
Puff Pancakes, 97
Pumpkin-Ginger Pancakes, 90
Scandinavian Apple Pancake, 120
Spice Pancakes with Lemon Sauce, 94
Whole Wheat Pancakes with Roasted Pecans,
 96

**Panko**
Parmesan Heirloom Cherry Tomatoes, 198

**Parfait**
Blueberry/Blackberry Yogurt Parfait, 38
Parmesan Heirloom Cherry Tomatoes, 198

**Parsley, Fresh**
Kiss My Grits!, 180
Mini Corn Cakes, 182
Parmesan Heirloom Cherry Tomatoes, 198
Peach-Nectarine Upside-Down French Toast,
 100

**Peaches**
Baked Apricots, 14
Birchermuesli, 40
Caramel Peach Bread Pudding, 116
Chilled Peach Soup, 34

Grilled Peaches or Nectarines, 31
Peach-Nectarine Upside-Down French Toast,
 100
Spiced Peach Compote, 32

**Peach Schnapps**
Ray's Strawberry Soup, 37
Pear Pecan Cardamom Bread, 69

**Pears**
Cranberry-Raspberry Poached Pears, 18
Pear Pecan Cardamom Bread, 69
Poached Pears with Orange Glaze, 16
Pomegranate Pear Salad, or Winter Fruit
 Salad, 13

**Pecans**
Blueberry Pecan Waffles, 110
Bourbon Pecan Syrup, 214
Caramel Peach Bread Pudding, 116
Gourmet Granola, 208
Pear Pecan Cardamom Bread, 69
Whole Wheat Pancakes with Roasted Pecans,
 96

**Peppers, Bell Sweet**
Garden Baked Eggs, 150
Mini Corn Cakes, 182
Potato Veggie Pancakes, 167
Shakshouka Flatbread, 176
Tri-Color Terrine, 130
Veggie Frittata, 133
Wake-Me-Up Salsa, 204

**Pie**
Maryland Blue Crab Quiche, 142
Northwest Salmon Breakfast Pie, 145
Tomato Basil Pie, 136
Pineapple Napoleon, 22
Pineapple Sunrise, 25

**Pineapple**

Birchermuesli, 40

Outrageously Great Waffles—with Flavor
Options, 106

Pineapple Napoleon, 22

Pineapple Sunrise, 25

**Plums**

Baked Apricots, 14

Stewed Plums, 29

Poached Pears with Orange Glaze, 16

**Polenta**

Creamy Polenta or Grits, 196

Pomegranate Ginger Muffins, 50

Pomegranate Pear Salad, or Winter Fruit Salad,
13

**Pomegranates**

Pomegranate Ginger Muffins, 50

Pomegranate Pear Salad, or Winter Fruit
Salad, 13

**Poppy Seeds**

Melodious Poppy Seed Bread, 72

Potato Galette, 194

Potato Veggie Pancakes, 167

**Potatoes**

Neapolitan Potatoes, 192

Potato Galette, 194

Potato Veggie Pancakes, 167

Roasted Fall Root Vegetables, 201

**Potatoes, Sweet**

Sweet Potato Hash, 190

**Prosciutto**

Ham, Apple, and Goat Cheese Breakfast Toast,
189

Huevos Trifecta, 156

**Pudding**

Blueberry Bread Pudding with Orange
Custard, 118

Caramel Peach Bread Pudding, 116

Mushroom Sausage Bread Pudding, 178

Puff Pancakes, 97

Pumpkin Bread, 70

Pumpkin-Ginger Pancakes, 90

Pumpkin Soup, 202

**Pumpkin**

Pumpkin Bread, 70

Pumpkin-Ginger Pancakes, 90

Pumpkin Soup, 202

Sunflower Pumpkin Bread, 71

*Blueberry Cornmeal Pancakes, 87*

**Quiche**
Asparagus Goat Cheese Crustless Quiche, 139
Maryland Blue Crab Quiche, 142
Mediterranean Quiche, 140
Spinach Brownies, 183

Raised Waffles, 108
**Raisins**
Birchermuesli, 40
Ginger Spice Pancakes, 92
Gourmet Granola, 208
Oatmeal Granola Muffins, 55
**Raspberry Juice**
Cranberry-Raspberry Poached Pears, 18
Ray's Strawberry Soup, 37
**Red Beets**  *See Beets, Red*
**Rhubarb**
Strawberry Rhubarb Coffee Cake, 64
Roasted Fall Root Vegetables, 201
**Roasted Red Peppers**
Mediterranean Quiche, 140
**Rolls**
Lemon Ginger Rolls, 78
**Rum**
Hot Apple Cider, 233
Outrageously Great Waffles—with Flavor
Options, 106

S

**Salad**
Pomegranate Pear Salad, or Winter Fruit
Salad, 13
**Salmon**
Northwest Salmon Breakfast Pie, 145
**Salmon, Smoked**
Smoked Salmon Avocado Toast, 166
Smoked Salmon Eggs Benedict, 163
**Salsa**
Black Bean and Tortilla Strata, 170
Corn, Tomato, Beet, and Basil Salsa, 207
Strawberry Salsa, 205
Wake-Me-Up Salsa, 204
**Sandwiches**
Grilled Cheese Bacon-Avocado-Tomato
Sandwich (aka "Cheese & BAT"), 165
**Sauces**
Arkansas Chocolate Gravy, 217
Blueberry Sauce, 218
Caramel Sauce, 215
Crème Fraîche, 222
Hot Water Hollandaise, 226
Lemon Sauce, 89, 219
Vanilla Sauce, 216
**Sausage**
Apple Sausage Bake, 188
Huevos Trifecta, 156
Kiss My Grits!, 180
Mushroom Sausage Bread Pudding, 178
Southwest Sausage Strata, 168
Sweet Potato Hash, 190

**Scallions**

Potato Veggie Pancakes, 167

Scandinavian Apple Pancake, 120

**Scones**

Fig and Kumquat Scones, 59

White Chocolate and Cranberry Tea Scones, 57

**Scrambled Eggs**

Basil and Tomato Egg Scramble, 159

**Semolina**

Shakshouka Flatbread, 176

**Sesame Seeds**

Gourmet Granola, 208

Shakshouka Flatbread, 176

**Shallots**

Fondue Florentine Soufflé, 148

Tri-Color Terrine, 130

Shoofly Pie Muffins, 56

Smoked Salmon Avocado Toast, 166

Smoked Salmon Eggs Benedict, 163

**Smoothie**

Berry Smoothie, 231

Some Like It… Cold! Cold-Brewed Iced Coffee, 232

**Soufflé**

Fondue Florentine Soufflé, 148

Spinach and Leek Soufflé, 146

**Soups**

Chilled Peach Soup, 34

Pumpkin Soup, 202

Ray's Strawberry Soup, 37

**Sour Cream**

Blueberry Sour Cream Pancakes with Lemon Sauce, 88

Southwest Sausage Strata, 168

Spiced Peach Compote, 32

Spice Pancakes with Lemon Sauce, 94

Spinach and Leek Soufflé, 146

Spinach Brownies, 183

**Spinach**

Fondue Florentine Soufflé, 148

Mediterranean Quiche, 140

Mushroom Crepes with Shiitake & Spinach Sauce, 174

Omelet with Variations, 124

Spinach and Leek Soufflé, 146

Veggie Frittata, 133

**Spinach, Frozen**

Spinach Brownies, 183

**Squash, Butternut**

Pumpkin Soup, 202

**Squash, Summer**

Roasted Fall Root Vegetables, 201

**Squash, Yellow**

Garden Baked Eggs, 150

Potato Veggie Pancakes, 167

Stewed Plums, 29

Strawberry Cornmeal Muffins, 53

Strawberry Rhubarb Coffee Cake, 64

Strawberry Salsa, 205

**Strawberries**

Baked Oatmeal, 112

Birchermuesli, 40

Decadent Chocolate French Toast with Strawberry Syrup, 104

Ray's Strawberry Soup, 37

Strawberry Cornmeal Muffins, 53

Strawberry Rhubarb Coffee Cake, 64

Strawberry Salsa, 205

Streusel Toppings, 47

Summer Frittata, 134

**Summer Squash** *See Squash, Summer*

**Sundried Tomatoes**
  Garden Baked Eggs, 150
Sunflower Pumpkin Bread, 71
**Sunflower Seeds**
  Gourmet Granola, 208
  Sunflower Pumpkin Bread, 71
Sunny Morning Citrus, 15
Sweet Potato Hash, 190
**Sweet Potatoes**
  Sweet Potato Hash, 190
**Swiss Chard**
  Tri-Color Terrine, 130
**Syrups**
  Bourbon Pecan Syrup, 214
  Cinnamon Syrup, 93
  Versatile Simple Syrups, 212

Southwest Sausage Strata, 168
Summer Frittata, 134
Tomato Basil Pie, 136
Tomatoes Benedict, 160
Wake-Me-Up Salsa, 204
**Tomatoes, Cherry**
  Basil and Tomato Egg Scramble, 159
  Parmesan Heirloom Cherry Tomatoes, 198
  Strawberry Salsa, 205
**Tortillas**
  Black Bean and Tortilla Strata, 170
  Breakfast Burrito, 172
  Southwest Sausage Strata, 168
Tri-Color Terrine, 130
**Triple Sec**
  Blueberry Bread Pudding with Orange
    Custard, 118

T

**Terrine**
  Tri-Color Terrine, 130
**Toast, French**  *See French Toast*
Tomato Basil Pie, 136
Tomatoes Benedict, 160
**Tomatoes**
  Breakfast Burrito, 172
  Corn, Tomato, Beet, and Basil Salsa, 207
  Grilled Cheese Bacon-Avocado-Tomato
    Sandwich (aka "Cheese & BAT"), 165
  Huevos Trifecta, 156
  Neapolitan Potatoes, 192
  Potato Galette, 194
  Shakshouka Flatbread, 176

*Parmesan Heirloom Cherry Tomatoes, 198*

## U

Upside-Down Sour Cherry Muffins, 48

## V

Vanilla Sauce, 216
**Vanilla**
  Vanilla Sauce, 216
Veggie Frittata, 133
Versatile Simple Syrups, 212

## W

**Waffles**
  Blueberry Pecan Waffles, 110
  Outrageously Great Waffles—with Flavor
    Options, 106
  Raised Waffles, 108
Wake-Me-Up Salsa, 204
**Walnuts**
  Apricot Walnut Muffins, 45
  Birchermuesli, 40
  Cranberry-Orange Bread, 66
  Gourmet Granola, 208
  Pumpkin Bread, 70
  Sunflower Pumpkin Bread, 71
**Watermelon**
  Grilled Watermelon Topped with Mango Salsa
    and Crème Fraîche, 26
  Mango Tango, 21

White Chocolate and Cranberry Tea Scones, 57
**Whole Wheat**
  Whole Wheat Pancakes with Roasted Pecans, 96
**Wine, Red**
  Cranberry-Raspberry Poached Pears, 18
  Hot Apple Cider, 233
**Wine, White**
  Mushroom Crepes with Shiitake & Spinach
    Sauce, 174

## Y

**Yellow Squash**  *See Squash, Yellow*

## Z

**Zucchini**
  Garden Baked Eggs, 150
  Potato Veggie Pancakes, 167
  Roasted Fall Root Vegetables, 201
  Summer Frittata, 134